A Magnificent Exchange

A Magnificent Exchange

◆

(Subara Shii Kokusai Koryu)

*Two Years in the Life of
an American Family in Japan*

Stephanie Allen-Adams

iUniverse, Inc.
New York Lincoln Shanghai

A Magnificent Exchange
(Subara Shii Kokusai Koryu)

iUniverse books may be ordered through booksellers or by contacting:

iUniverse
2021 Pine Lake Road, Suite 100
Lincoln, NE 68512
www.iuniverse.com
1-800-Authors (1-800-288-4677)

ISBN-13: 978-0-595-37698-8 (pbk)
ISBN-13: 978-0-595-82081-8 (ebk)
ISBN-10: 0-595-37698-3 (pbk)
ISBN-10: 0-595-82081-6 (ebk)

Printed in the United States of America

To our good friend Charles, who lived life to the fullest and enjoyed each day as if it would be his last.

For all those who have ever struggled to understand, and all those who have struggled to *be* understood.

"If your mind is empty, it is always ready for anything; it is open to anything. In the beginner's mind there are many possibilities; in the expert's mind there are few."

—*Shunryu Suzuki*

This book is about crossing cultures, following dreams and changing lives. Over time it moves from cultural fear to culture shock to cultural understanding. It's a story of hope, strength and resiliency. I hope that those who read it will find it enlightening, encouraging and entertaining and that they too will be empowered and encouraged to follow *their* dreams. I also hope that our story will help to uplift the spirit and inspire the soul.

Contents

Part III   *Going Home Again (Kikoku)*

Acknowledgments

With much love, gratitude and appreciation, I fondly dedicate this book to Christopher Allen-Bradley, James E. Adams, Monica Adams, Erika Maxie, Eric Maxie, James Dennison and family, John Allen and family, Maxie Allen and family, Joseph Allen and family, the Lewis Family, Florence Joseph and family, Florence Adams, Alicia Parham, Charles Parham and family, Viola Williams, JoAnna Hobson, Michela Floyd, Rothwell Floyd, Miyoko Kawakita-Wordell, Mariko Wordell, Sachiko Nishimura, Hiroshi Nishimura, Keiko Sugi, Miki Kawahashi, Kume Kim, Keiko Toyoda, Barbara Larson, Lillian Sugarman, Audrey Siler, Joan Alofs, Eileen Albright, Debbi Sorrentino, Cindy Graham, Marianna Thiebaud, Gail Slocum, Victoria Steinman, Nancy Condit, Sue Kane, Pam Weaver, Kellye Abernathy, Alistair F. Bruce, Erica Taylor, Shenaz Popat, Corene Samerson and Shawna Ridley. I give special thanks to my loving mother, Margaret Allen, who has always supported my efforts and has encouraged me to follow my dreams.

Prologue

Chicago; "The Windy City;" my hometown. Known throughout the world as "the great metropolis of the mid-west," it's nestled neatly along the shores of Lake Michigan and boasts of its "Magnificent Mile," incredible nightlife, an unmistakable skyline, rich sounds of jazz, gospel and blues and the mouth-watering aromas of award-winning barbecue and "Chicago-style deep dish pizza."

Chicago also prides itself in being a city that's home to various colorful, vibrant, and ethnically rich communities. However, in these communities, as fabulous as they were, its individuals have not always peacefully co-existed. In these communities, cultures have sometimes crossed; sometimes merged and more often than not; have even collided.

◆   ◆   ◆

I was born in Chicago in 1952, the only daughter and the youngest of five children born to Margaret and Eugene. My life was good; it was happy, that is, until my father suddenly passed away from cancer four years later. The year was 1956. Everything suddenly changed. My mother was in a state of shock; my brothers were confused; and I was just frightened. I learned just how quickly things can change. Within a matter of days, my mother had gone from being a wife, to being a widow. She had gone from having the support of my father, to having to support her family on her on. That couldn't have been easy. She was immediately thrust into a position where she had to suddenly grieve the loss of my father while trying to find the strength to maintain some semblance of household order. I didn't understand the situation then; I definitely understand it now.

Although I was only four years old when I lost my father, I can still remember him. He was my "friendly giant," so tall, so handsome and so kind. He had a melodious voice, a warm smile and a big booming laugh. I can remember how happy I was when he came home from work, walked through the door, swept me off my feet, wrapped me in his arms and showered me with hugs and kisses. I always felt so special when he was around. So, when I lost him, I felt like I'd lost my protector; my best friend. When my father passed away, our family dynamic suddenly changed. Our mother became "head of household" and my brothers had to take on more responsibility. They also became "self-appointed" protectors of my mother and of me. And all of sudden they felt they needed to look after "the baby of the family" (that would be me.) It was as if, overnight, I went from having "one" father, to having "four fathers."

Being the only girl (and the youngest) can have its advantages; but it can also have its challenges. The biggest challenge for me was that my brothers sometime forgot that their little sister (or "the baby of the family") would one day grow up. And although my "position" in the family would never change (I'd always be the youngest; I'd always be "the baby"), but I wouldn't always *be* a baby. What my brothers failed to realize was that one day I would grow up and be totally capable of taking care of myself and making my own decisions. On an intellectual level they understood that; on an emotional level, they did not.

◆   ◆   ◆

Shortly after my father's death, my mother made the decision to relocate our family to a new home, one outside of the city limits. She found a beautiful community of town homes on the far south side of the city called Altgeld Gardens. Altgeld Gardens was aptly named because it boasted of some of the most beautiful and colorful flowering gardens that I'd ever seen. It was a relatively new community (12 years old) that had been built to house African-American veterans who were returning from World War II and their families. We moved in when I was four years old and lived there for 13 years. It was longest I've lived in any one place.

Altgeld Gardens was a community where neighbors took pride in ownership and where families supported each other and looked out for each other. And like most communities in 1956, it was racially segregated and ethnically divided. The first time I was ever exposed to an Anglo-American was when my mother enrolled me in kindergarten at the local public school, that's where I met my teacher, Miss Rice. However, I wouldn't be exposed to a diverse student body for another 11 years (when I transferred from my neighborhood high school to a vocational school several miles north of my home.) It was during that time that I had an opportunity to be exposed to people, languages, and cultures that were different from my own. It was the first time that I had the opportunity to let go of some of my own prejudices and preconceived notions. It was the first time that my world became bigger than just my immediate community.

◆   ◆   ◆

Although I had limited exposure to diversity within my community, my mother saw to it that I be exposed to a world outside of the one I was growing up in. I have fond memories of her taking me on little excursions right within the city limits to visit other neighborhoods, cultural museums, concert halls, local cinemas, and the best part of all, to dine at nice restaurants. She'd always say to me, "The world is a big, beautiful place, don't limit yourself to only one small corner of it. Explore." Whether she realized it or not, her words stayed with me forever.

Chicago is a city known for its diverse population. However, during my childhood, it was a segregated city; one where people remained in their neighborhoods; didn't interact with each other and didn't mingle. Each ethnic group kept to themselves—"kept to their own kind." And there were "pockets" of ethnicity. As people emigrated from different foreign countries and settled in Chicago, they brought with them their own unique cultures; languages; music and foods, and they formed their own separate and unique communities. You can walk down any street on any given day and see street signs written in English and in the native languages of its inhabitants. One can hear languages other than English being spoken, see people dressed in their native attire, smell the different aromas cascading from restaurants and sidewalk cafes, and immediately feel like you've been suddenly transported to another place and time.

From an early age, I became fascinated with other peoples' cultures, languages and foods. So, it's no surprise that I would dream of one day traveling to, or even living in another part of the world. It had long been what I'd aspired to, however, the timing for travel never seemed quite right. When I had the time, I didn't have the money, and when I had the money, I didn't have the time. It would be almost 40 years before my dream will be realized.

◆   ◆   ◆

It was the fulfillment of that dream that became the inspiration for this story.

PART I

Going Abroad (Gaikoku ni Iku)

o o o o o o o o o o o o o o o o o o o o o o o o o o o o o o o o o o o

"You gain strength, courage and confidence by every experience in which you really stop to look fear in the face."

—*Eleanor Roosevelt*
www.quoteland.com

1

The formation of my gregarious personality, my open mind and my positive spirit is the result of having grown up in a loving environment where I felt supported, encouraged and valued. I was taught that "the sky was the limit" and that I could do anything that I put my mind to. As a result of all that positive reinforcement, I became someone who took chances and who had no fears. Well, that's not *completely* true, we all fear *something*. It's just that for me, I hadn't had an opportunity to know what it was that I feared. That is, not until 1992. What I had, I quickly discovered was "a fear of the unknown."

◆　　　◆　　　◆

Life as I'd known it was about to change forever. I was about to make a major decision and embark upon a journey that would forever change my life and the life of my young son. I went from fearing nothing (I thought), to fearing everything—a fear of flying, a fear of failure and a fear of being away from family and friends.

◆　　　◆　　　◆

I had no idea of just how haunting this new endeavor would be. And I found myself experiencing feelings of uneasiness and discontent. Although I'd been exposed to a diverse population for a very long time, somehow, this would be different; this would be much more challenging. A bevy of questions were going through my mind, "What if the Japanese don't warm up to me? What if my students are uncomfortable with me? What if I'm uncomfortable with them? How will we communicate?" And then there was Christopher. I gave a lot of thought to how this change would affect him. I asked myself, "How will he manage without his family and friends? How will he manage without his grandmother (whom he adores and who adores him?) How will he do in school? How will *he* communicate?" I really wondered if I was making a wise decision. I tried to rationalize by saying, "You're only going for one year. If you don't like it, or if Christopher doesn't like it, you can always come home."

This really was one of the most difficult decisions I'd ever made and although I was trying to be strong, it really was like "going out on a limb" with no supports. I had my reservations but I was still willing to take a chance. I really didn't want to spend the rest of my life with the regret of having said no.

◆   ◆   ◆

I was determined to conquer my "fear of the unknown" and to go forward on my new adventure with an open mind and a spirit that was free from any preconceived notions, any unrealistic expectations, assumptions or prejudices. I was determined to put aside my limited, one-sided, American way of thinking and make a concerted effort to see the world from a different perspective. I was excited about the prospect of learning about, understanding and respecting a new culture. I understood that I was traveling to Japan to *teach*, but I was also traveling there to *learn*.

So after months of convincing myself (and everyone else) that this was the right thing to do, I started making plans, and in the process, starting turning my fears into a challenge—and I love a challenge!

2

When I was four years old, I had to transition to a new life without my father. Now at 38 years old, I was in the process of making another major transition. And this time, like the time before, I had no idea what to expect.

It was the winter of 1991. I was a single mother living in Chicago with my five-year-old son Christopher, who was in kindergarten at the local Montessori school. He was in his third and final year of Montessori and in the fall he would be transitioning to first grade at a new school. He'd reached another milestone. He'd soon be saying goodbye to all his friends and to the only teachers he'd ever known. The transition would be difficult for him, but it would prove to be equally as difficult for me. He and I had grown accustomed to the safe, secure and nurturing environment that his school had provided for the past two and a half years. Starting over again in a new place wouldn't be easy.

◆   ◆   ◆

In 1988, two Montessori teachers interviewed local families to assess the need for a full-day Montessori school in our community. When I read in the local newspaper that plans to open a new Montessori school were underway, I immediately called the co-directors, introduced myself, told them I had a young son and that I too had been a Montessori teacher. They were very happy to hear from me. I told them that I was willing to do whatever I could to help facilitate the opening. I knew that if I volunteered my services, I could ensure that the school would be operational by Christopher's third birthday and he could attend.

As a former Montessori teacher myself, I understood better than anyone, the benefits of the "Montessori Method." I'd seen firsthand just how well young children thrived in that type of environment and I wanted no less for Christopher. So, if I could be instrumental in helping to get a school opened and operating, I was determined to do everything in my power to make that happen.

◆   ◆   ◆

After I graduated from college with a degree in Sociology, I had planned to return to graduate school and secure a Master's in Social Work and then find employment in a hospital or a clinical setting. But all that changed the day I walked into the career services office of my university and picked up a brochure on Montessori education. I'd never heard of Montessori, but I was intrigued by what I read. Dr. Maria Montessori was the first woman to graduate from the University of Rome in 1896. Upon graduation, she volunteered to work in the asylums for the insane where she encountered "feeble-minded" children who struggled to function or fit in at school and at home. She also encountered poor children from the slums of Rome who were left to care for themselves while their parents worked.

Dr. Montessori decided to take on the challenge of working with these children whom everyone deemed "unteachable" and create a method of education that could help them learn. She also created a series of self-correcting materials that would allow these children to correct their own mistakes and proceed at their own pace. She established *Casa di Bambini* (The Children's House) the first Montessori school in Italy.

In 1913, while at the height of her career, Dr. Montessori traveled to the U.S. and began establishing Montessori training centers throughout the U.S. and the world to help train teachers in "the method." In a Montessori classroom, children learn through activities that involve explorations, manipulatives, order, repetition and communication.

I contacted the local Montessori teachers' training center in Chicago and inquired about becoming a teacher myself. I was invited to visit and observe a Montessori classroom and to speak with the director. After seeing children at work in a Montessori classroom, my fate was sealed. I knew I'd found my new career. I enrolled in an intensive summer training program that was complete with lectures, presentations and extensive research. Following the summer-long course I worked as an intern (student teacher) in a classroom setting under the tutelage of an experienced teacher. Toward the end of my internship, I was observed by a Master teacher who evaluated my performance, and then I sat for a series of exams before receiving my certification.

Upon receiving certification, I taught at several Montessori schools throughout the city of Chicago and was soon struck by how elitist Montessori had become. From where I sat, it seemed that Montessori had become synonymous with affluence and privilege and that only the children from higher income homes were reaping the benefits of a Montessori education. Throughout my teaching career, I never had the opportunity to work with children from lower income homes or those with special needs as Dr. Montessori had intended. It was her compassion and her commitment to these special children that had attracted me to Montessori in the first place.

After several years of teaching, I decided to establish my own school so that I could reach "all" children; "all" families. I relocated from Chicago to a small community just east of Gary, Indiana (where my mother lived at the time.) I conducted a needs assessment of the community, interviewed local families and contacted social service agencies to inquire if there was a need for (or an interest in) a Montessori school. Everyone I spoke with was very excited about the prospect. I arranged a meeting with the pastor and congregation at the local Lutheran Church; told them of my interest in establishing a Montessori school and proposed renting space in their annex. They loved the idea and thought that a Montessori school would be a great addition to the community and it would provide added revenue for the church. We agreed on a monthly fee; I submitted a proposal, and we signed a one year contract. I made arrangements for a state inspection; applied for a state license; purchased supplies and equipment; and opened my school right in the heart of a working class community east of Gary, Indiana. On the first day, I opened my doors with only two children. But word quickly spread throughout the community and within three months of operation, enrolled swelled to full capacity—33 children. I offered a full-day Montessori program for 3-6 year olds and a before and after school program for 6-12 year olds. By establishing myself in a working class community and by accommodating children with special needs and those who were struggling at home and in other programs, I remained true to the spirit of Dr. Montessori. My tuition was based on a "sliding scale" (which meant that families with lower incomes paid what they could afford.) My dream was for my school to be accessible to, and affordable for "all" who chose to attend.

At age 29, I had a personal sense of pride. I was proud because I felt like I was making a difference in the lives of children and their families; and proud because of what I'd accomplished before the age of 30. The hours I devoted to my work were long and hard, but extremely rewarding because the establishment of my own Montessori was a "labor of love" and a "dream come true."

◆   ◆   ◆

Owning and operating a school in a working class community had its benefits, but it also had its shortfalls. That meant, whenever a family member lost his or her job due to layoffs or cutbacks; I lost a student. Unfortunately, with an increase in layoffs, meant a decrease in enrollment. Within five years, my enrollment dwindled from 33 children to an all-time low of only five. The year was 1986 and by then Christopher was born. I could no longer afford to keep the school open. Sadly, I was forced to close my doors—up to that point, one of the hardest things I'd ever had to do. I was absolutely devastated; I was sad; I was heart-broken. I felt like I'd disappointed an entire community. But my spirit was lifted when all the families banned together for the last time to say goodbye and to celebrate me and my efforts. They assured me that it was the *school* that had failed; not *me*. They thanked me for my contributions to their children and to the community and they wished me well.

I sold my house, packed my bags and moved back to Chicago. I was forced to find a job that paid a substantial salary so I could afford to support myself and my son—unfortunately, that wouldn't be as a Montessori teacher.

◆   ◆   ◆

The year was 1988 when I first met the two co-directors who would eventually open the Montessori school that Christopher would attend. It had been over two years since I'd closed my school and over two years since I'd taught. However, I was no less passionate about Montessori and no less committed to the Montessori Method.

As a working mom, I needed a full-day program, but none of the schools in our neighborhood offered full-day. So when I read in the local newspaper that a new full-day Montessori school would be opening, I was absolutely thrilled.

◆   ◆   ◆

I called Anna Spencer and Jean Anderson and asked if I could make an appointment to meet them and tour the building.

"Hello."

"Hello. May I speak with Anna Spencer or Jean Anderson?"

"This is Anna Spencer."

"Ms. Spencer, my name is Stephanie Allen. I read in the local newspaper that you and Jean Anderson will be opening a new Montessori school."

"Yes we will. It should be opening in the spring."

"I'm the parent of a two and a half year old. I'm also a former Montessori teacher. The reason for my call is to ask if there is anything I can do to help you in getting the school opened on time."

"This is wonderful. We can use all the help we can get. Would you like to come by and meet us and tour the building?"

"I would love to."

"The address is 4800 Avers Avenue. Is tomorrow at 6:00 PM good for you?"

"That's good. I'll just come by tomorrow after work."

"We'll see you then."

"Goodbye."

"Goodbye."

◆   ◆   ◆

Christopher and I arrived at the school the following evening. We rang the doorbell and were greeted by Anna and Jean. Anna was a short, petite African-American woman with beautiful, smooth, caramel-colored skin. She wore tiny red reading glasses and her silver-gray hair was styled in a short, curly Afro. Jean was a tall, slim, attractive woman of Anglo-European descent. She had long brown hair and piercing blue eyes. Anna and Jean had taught at the same Montessori school for years and had become best friends. They said they were fulfilling a lifelong dream by having plans to own and operate their own Montessori school.

"Welcome Stephanie. This must be Christopher. Please come in."

"Thank you. It's so nice to me you both."

"It's so nice to meet both of you. We were so excited to hear from you."

"You don't know how happy I was to read that you were opening a Montessori school, just in time for Christopher to attend."

"It seems like we'll all benefit."

"You're absolutely right. Just let me know what I can do, and when you need me to start."

"Would you be interested in serving on our advisory board as the parent representative?"

"I'd love to serve. What's involved in that?"

"You'll be expected to attend monthly board meetings, and be in the rotation for taking notes and then submitting minutes."

"I can do that."

"That's great."

I toured the facility; we talked for about an hour, and then we exchanged telephone numbers and made plans to meet again.

◆　　　◆　　　◆

Although I had a "volunteer spirit," I'd never been so excited and so committed to a project. I helped out with cleaning, painting, and gardening and with setting up classrooms. I worked in the office answering telephones, making copies and mailing out enrollment forms. I also served as the school's "unofficial" public relations representative. I told everyone I met about the new school. I was motivated to do everything within my power to ensure that the school would open in time for Christopher's third birthday so he could attend.

The Montessori School of Hyde Park opened its doors on the first day of March in 1989. Christopher was enrolled as the very first student. Within a week seven families had enrolled and within a few months, we'd grown to 12! As word spread throughout the community, enrollment was at full capacity within a year. Two new teachers were hired to work along side Jean and Anna, and before long, the school had a waiting list! For the entire three years that Christopher attended, I volunteered as a board member and I filled in as a substitute teacher.

◆　　　◆　　　◆

By the winter of 1991 Christopher was four years old. He was in his second year at Montessori and would soon be entering his third and final year at the school. It was time for me to begin the search for a new school for first grade. Christopher was a child who struggled with change. I was a mom who struggled with informing him that a change was about to take place.

It seemed that he'd just made a full transition to Montessori and had just become comfortable with his teachers, his friends and his routine, and now he was preparing for yet another change. As an adult, I could intellectualize that change is part of life, but as a five-year-old, Christopher could not.

3

Little did I know at the time, but our lives were about to make a 360 degree change.

One evening following an advisory board meeting, Anna approached me with a most curious question.

"Stephanie, do you know of anyone who might be interested in traveling to Japan to teach in an International Montessori Language School for one year?"

Half jokingly, I said, "Maybe me!"

"I didn't think of you. I guess I didn't think you'd be interested. But if you are, maybe I can make arrangements for you to meet my friend Kanako when she arrives here in a few days?"

"That would be great. I'd love to meet her."

Anna told me that her friend lived in Yokkaichi, Japan. They'd met when Kanako was living in the U.S. and training to become a Montessori teacher under Anna's tutelage. Her last name was Winston (her husband Sam was American). Kanako and Sam had met when they were students at The University of Illinois. They married soon thereafter and now had a 12 year-old daughter named Yumi. When they returned to Japan, Kanako established a Montessori International Language School and Sam secured a teaching position at Nanzan University in Nagoya.

"So, Anna, are you telling me that your friend travels to the U.S. to recruit teachers to work in her school?"

"Not necessarily. Her in-laws live in Chicago, so she travels here to visit them. But while here she makes good use of her time by also keeping an eye open for qualified teachers."

"Does she usually confine her search to Chicago?"

"No. Not really. It's just that she was fortunate enough to find a teacher here last year, so she thought she'd try again."

"So, she has someone working at her school right now?"

"That's right. If you'd like, I can arrange a meeting."

"I'll tell you what, you let me know when she arrives, and then we can work something out."

"I'll do that."

◆   ◆   ◆

Within a week, Kanako arrived from Japan and I made plans to meet her. She was waiting at the school one evening when I arrived to pick up Christopher. When I rang the doorbell, she arrived at the door with Anna.

Anna introduced us. "Kanako, I'd like you to meet our friend Stephanie. She's our parent volunteer extraordinaire and she also serves on our advisory board. She's a true "friend of the school."

"Anna, you embarrass me."

"I don't mean to embarrass you. But Jean and I really do appreciate all that you do."

"Well thank you. I do it because Christopher's happy here and I love this school."

I looked at Kanako and was surprised at how tall she was. When I walked in, we looked at each other (almost eye-to-eye.) I'm 5 feet 9 inches; she was at least 5 feet 6 inches! She had a beautiful round face and wore large aviator-style glasses. Her black hair was streaked with gray and was styled in a medium-length bob with bangs. She was dressed nicely (but conservatively) in black slacks and sweater with a red button-down shirt layered underneath and black loafers.

"Stephanie, I'm pleased to meet you."

"Kanako, I'm pleased to meet you too."

Anna said, "Enjoy your meeting and don't worry about Christopher. We'll give him a snack and keep him busy while the two you sit down and talk."

"Thank you Anna. I really appreciate that."

When we sat down, Kanako said, "Stephanie, I wanted you to know that I'm looking for a teacher, not for this year, but for next year. I'm currently working with a Montessori teacher from right here in Chicago. She took a one-year sabbatical from her job so she could travel to Japan and teach. She's approaching the end of her contract and will be returning to Chicago to resume her teaching job next year. I'm looking to recruit a teacher for next school year. Do you think this is something you'd be interested in?"

"I can't really say yet, I honestly don't know."

"What is your job now?"

"I work for The University of Illinois Cooperative Extension Service where I coordinate after school programs in the city parks. Unfortunately, my program is a two-year "pilot" program which means it's operating on federal grant money. So, when the money runs out, the program comes to an end, as does my employment. And when that happens, I could be open to most anything—even teaching in Japan."

"That's good to know."

We talked for what seemed like hours. She wanted to know all about me.

"Stephanie, did you grow up here in Chicago?"

"I did. I've lived here my entire life (except for the five years that I lived in Indiana before Christopher was born.)

"I do love Chicago", she said. "It's one of my favorite cities."

"Kanako, did you grow up in Yokkaichi?"

"I did. I've lived there all life except for the few years that I lived in the U.S. when I went to college. I have a younger sister named Fumie. She's married and has two young children. She and her family live with our parents, in our childhood home. My father is a rice farmer and my mother works at home full-time. I attended Japanese schools throughout high school. However, upon graduation, I traveled to the U.S. so I could attend an American university and increase my English proficiency. I met my husband Sam while we were both university students. After graduation, we continued our studies. I enrolled in the teacher training program to secure my Montessori teaching certificate; my husband Sam enrolled in graduate school. We got married and we now have a 12 year-old daughter named Yumi."

"Does Yumi speak English?"

"Yes. She's bi-lingual. She speaks English and Japanese. She also has dual citizenship (U.S. and Japanese.)"

"That's great. I'm impressed."

◆　　　◆　　　◆

Kanako and I had so many questions of each other and so little time. One of the first questions I asked (which was a major concern for me) was "What about Christopher?"

"Kanako, have you ever hired a teacher with a child?"

"No I haven't."

"Would you consider it?"

"I've never thought about it, but I would take it under advisement. I'm sure that having a child on board will pose some unseen challenges, but I'm not averse to hiring a teacher with a child. I'm sure we can work something out."

"I have to be honest with you. The thought of relocating overseas and taking along a young child—that really frightens me."

"I'm sure it does. But you know what? You don't have to make a decision right now. We're just in the "talking stage. You have plenty of time to think about this."

"Kanako, I hesitate to ask this question, but I feel like I must."

"Go ahead."

"How do you think the Japanese would respond to Christopher and me—I mean, being "Americans of Color"?

"That's a fair question. And I'll answer it by saying that the Japanese (especially those who live in Yokkaichi) haven't really had many opportunities to interact with Americans outside of those of Anglo-European descent. But, having said that, I don't think you or Christopher will have any problems."

"Are you sure?"

"Well, I'm not sure, but I don't think it'll be an issue at all."

"That's good to know."

"I'll tell you what, because we both have a lot to think about and a lot to talk about, let's *keep* talking. I'll be in Chicago for several more days. If you have any more questions or concerns, just give me a call and we'll talk about it."

"Let's do that."

"And Stephanie, do you think you can bring a copy of your resume to the school tomorrow?"

"I can do that."

"I'll stop by and pick it up from Anna."

"Once again, it was so nice meeting you. We'll talk again."

"It was nice meeting you too."

"Goodnight."

"Goodnight."

♦   ♦   ♦

My meeting with Kanako had gone extremely well and I'd really enjoyed meeting her. I went back to work; Christopher went back to school and I didn't give much more thought to Japan one way or the other. But then, one evening in April, 1992 while Christopher and I were having dinner, our telephone rang. Normally, I'd never interrupt our dinner by answering. I'd let the answering machine answer then return the call after dinner. However, this time, something told me to answer. I said, "Excuse me Christopher." I went to answer,

"Hello."

"Hello. This is Kanako from Japan. Do you remember me?"

I couldn't believe my ears.

"Of course I remember you. How are you?"

"I'm fine. How are you?"

"I'm doing great."

"I'm calling to see if you've given any more thought to coming to Japan to teach?"

My contract with The University of Illinois Cooperative Extension Service would be coming to an end in a matter of months, so with the thought of unemployment looming large in my mind and with no prospects on the horizon, there wasn't much to think about.

"Yes, I've thought about it, and I'm thrilled to know that you're still interested in talking to me. But tell me, have *you* given anymore thought to a teacher with a child?"

"Do you have time to talk about it?"

"Christopher and I were just having dinner. Do you think you can call me back in an hour?"

"I'll be happy to call you back."

I returned to the table.

"Who was that mommy?"

"That was Kanako, my friend from Japan. Do you remember her?"

"Yes. She came to my school."

"That's right. She sure did."

"Why is she calling you?"

"She'd like to talk to me about coming to her school in Japan to teach."

"Can I go too?"

"Of course you can. If I decide to go, you'll go too."

Just as we'd finished dinner and cleared the kitchen, the telephone rang again.

"Hello."

"Hello. Is this a good time for you to talk?"

"Yes, it is. Christopher and I have just finished eating dinner."

"So, Stephanie, do you have any more questions about Japan?"

"First of all, I have to say that I was really surprised to hear from you. I really didn't know how serious you were about having me come to Japan I wasn't sure that I'd hear from you again."

"I was indeed serious. After we talked, I thought a lot about you. And I thought you might be good for my school."

"So tell me, do you have any questions?"

"As a matter of fact I do. When do you need us to come there?"

"The end of August would be good."

"That doesn't give us much time. This is April already."

"I know. That only gives you four months. But you can do it."

"Kanako, you know, I've never traveled outside of the U.S. and I have to tell you that the thought of traveling overseas makes me very nervous."

"It can be a bit daunting, but I'll help you with whatever you need. Trust me, you'll be fine. I'll work with you every step of the way. The first thing you'll need to do is contact my travel agent in Los Angeles and make your travel arrangements. After that, you'll need to get passport photos and passports. Once you get those things done, call me and we'll talk again. Meanwhile, if you don't mind, I can have my husband Sam give you a call. He might be able to answer some of the questions that I can't."

"That would be great. That way, if I have any last minute questions, I can talk to him. Thank you Kanako."

"You're welcome. I'm glad you've decided to come."

"I'm happy to know that you're still interested in me."

◆   ◆   ◆

The following evening Christopher and I were sitting in front of the fireplace reading a bedtime story when the telephone rang. Normally, I wouldn't interrupt our story time either, but I was expecting Sam's call, so this time I made an exception and picked up.

"Hello."

"Hello. This is Sam, Kanako's husband. She told me to call you. Is this a good time for you to talk?"

"It is Sam. Thank you so much for calling."

Sam had a nice, calm, soothing voice that immediately put me at ease. He also had a great sense of humor.

"Sam, I hope you don't mind, but I have a whole list of questions for you."

"I don't mind at all. That's why I called. I know that relocation can be stressful, especially if you're relocating to a different part of the world. I've been where you are right now, so I definitely understand how you feel."

"Sam, I have to tell you that I'm really nervous about coming to Japan. I don't really know what to expect."

"Stephanie, that's perfectly understandable. Like I said, I've been in your shoes. If it will make you feel any better, please know that the people of Japan are the most accommodating and the most gracious people you'll ever meet. I guarantee you that you and Christopher will feel like you're at home in no time at all. Plus, everyone's looking forward to your arrival."

"Thank you Sam. That does make me feel much better."

"I'm glad to know that."

"So Sam, tell me, what do you do in Japan?"

"I'm a Professor of English Language at Nanzan University in Nagoya."

"That sounds impressive. Do you like it?"

"I love it. The students are great."

"You're lucky. Anyone who loves their job is lucky."

"What do you do in your spare time?"

"I enjoy research and writing. I also enjoy traveling and singing and playing guitar."

"You sing and play guitar?"

"I do. I'm not very good, but I enjoy myself a lot."

"Believe it or not, I sing and play also."

"Well, we'll just have to get together and perform a little duet sometime."

"That sounds great. I look forward to it."

"Sam, I hope you don't mind, but I have one more question for you."

"What is it?"

"What would you suggest that I bring from home for Christopher and for me? You know, the kinds of things that we might not be able to buy in Japan."

"I would suggest that you bring some of your favorite music and definitely bring some of Christopher's favorite toys and books. You'll soon realize that you can buy most anything here. However, if I were you, I'd start with the music and the toys and books."

"I appreciate knowing that. Thank you."

"I'm glad I could be of service to you. And I look forward to meeting you and Christopher. Kanako has told us at lot about the both of you."

"I look forward to meeting you and Yumi. We've heard a lot about you also."

"Stephanie, it's been nice talking to you."

"It's been so nice talking to you also. And thank you again for calling."

"It's been my pleasure." And if you have any more questions, please don't hesitate to call us."

"Thank you again."

"Goodnight."

"Goodnight."

◆   ◆   ◆

The following morning I was still reeling from the excitement. I had to pinch myself. "Am I dreaming?" I said to myself, "I can't believe that Christopher and I will be going to Japan in a matter of months!" I couldn't wait to call Kanako's agent, but then I remembered that he was in California which was three hours behind Chicago time. I patiently waited until 12:00 noon. Right at noon, I dialed The Mira Vista Travel Agency.

"Good morning. This is Mira Vista Travel."

"Good morning. Is this Mr. Goldman?"

"Yes, it is."

"Mr. Goldman, my name is Stephanie Allen. I'm Kanako Winston's friend. She told me to call you to make travel arrangements for travel to Japan."

"I've been waiting for your call. What can I do for you?"

"My son and I will travel to Nagoya on 22 August."

"How old is your son?"

"He's six years-old."

"When do you plan to return to Chicago?"

"We plan to return in one year."

"I'll take care of your reservations right away. And if you have any questions, please don't hesitate to call me or my assistant, Sarah."

"Thank you, Mr. Goldman. I look forward to hearing from you."

"I or Sarah will call you within a week."

"Goodbye."

"Goodbye."

Now that our travel arrangements were underway, my next order of business was to start informing family, friends and our landlord about our plans to relocate.

4

Feelings of excitement mixed with anxiety equaled stress. The summer of 1992 was a summer like no other, before or since. Christopher and I were about to embark upon an incredible journey that would forever change our lives.

I needed to have our plans confirmed and to be absolutely sure that it would happen before I started breaking the news to everyone. Of course, my mother was the first person I called.

"Hello mother."

"Hello darling. How are you?"

"I'm doing great."

"How's my Christopher?"

"He's doing great too."

"I've got some exciting news to share with you."

"What is it?"

"Christopher and I have been invited to live in Japan for a year."

"Really?"

"How did that come about?"

"Christopher's teacher introduced me to her friend from Japan. She was in the U.S. to visit family and to begin recruitment for a teacher. I met with her, we talked and after several months, she called me with an offer."

"Steph, I think that's great!"

"When will you leave?"

"We'll be leaving at the end of August."

"Oh my, that's only four months from now!"

"I know. August will be here before you know it."

"You know that I'll miss you and Christopher so much, but I'm so happy for you."

"Thank, you mother. This is such an incredible opportunity, I just couldn't say no."

"No hon, I wouldn't want you to say no."

"I knew you'd be happy for us. So, you think I've made the right decision?"

"Believe me dear, you have."

Talking to my mom had always been easy. Since I was child, she'd always encouraged me and had always supported my efforts. This time was no different.

Now I had to start placing calls to my brothers—all four of them. Based on past experience, I knew that breaking the news to them wouldn't be easy, and they probably wouldn't be as supportive or as enthusiastic as my mother had been. I was right. But I still had to call. I called my oldest brother first. He had no hesitation about expressing his concerns over me taking Christopher and leaving the country.

"Hello."

"Hello Jason."

"Hello little sis, how are you?"

"I'm doing great. How're you?"

"I'm doing great too. To what do I owe this honor?"

"I've got some news."

"Oh really? What is it?"

"I've been invited to go to Japan and teach for a year."

"What?"

"That's right."

"Little sis, have you given this serious thought?"

"I have. I've thought long and hard about this."

"What about Christopher's education?"

"He's young and children are resilient. I'm sure he'll do just fine."

"Who do you know in Japan?"

"No one yet, except for Kanako. She's the one who's invited me to teach in her school. But I'm sure we'll meet lots of people."

"How long are you planning to stay?"

"Like I said, just for a year. We'll be back before you know it."

"Do you think this is a wise thing to do?"

"I do. Plus, I'll be out of work anyway in August. So, going to Japan to work is as good as going anywhere. And, I think it's an incredible opportunity. Don't worry so much. We'll be just fine."

I telephoned the other three brothers and got pretty much the same reaction. They all thought my decision was pretty far-fetched. But, overall, I wasn't really surprised at their reaction; they were simply doing what they'd always done. In their minds, they were simply trying to protect me; trying to look out for my best interest. My age didn't matter, to them, I was still their little sis; I was still "the baby of the family."

Next, I called my best friend, Cecilia. She expressed more concern than my family.

"Stephanie, have you lost your mind?"

"No, my mind is completely intact."

"Don't you think you're being a bit impulsive?"

"I'm not being impulsive at all. This is not a decision I made in haste, it's been in the works for quite some time now."

"What about Christopher?"

"I have no idea how well he'll adjust, but I'm sure he'll be OK. As long as he has me, he'll be fine."

"Stephanie, I must say, I really admire your sense of daring. I could never just pack it all up and relocate to a foreign country. I *wish* I could, but I wouldn't have the nerve."

"Look at it this way, Cecilia. We're only going over for a year. If things don't work out, we can always come home.

"You're right."

"Congratulations, and good luck my friend."

"Thank you Cecilia. And don't worry so much. We'll be just fine."

◆   ◆   ◆

The following day I called my landlord, Mr. Hobbs.

"Hello Mr. Hobbs, this is Stephanie Allen. How are you?"

"I'm fine Stephanie. How are you?"

"I'm doing well thank you."

"That's very good. What can I do for you?"

"Mr. Hobbs, I wanted you to know that Christopher and I will be relocating to Japan."

"Is that right? To Japan, huh?"

"Yes sir. We're going to Japan."

"When are you planning to leave?"

"We're planning to leave at the end of August."

And spoken like a true businessman, the next words out of his mouth were,

"You are aware that you've signed a lease that you're legally bound to and that by law you're responsible for payments until the end of that lease right?"

"Yes, Mr. Hobbs, I'm fully aware of that. That's why I'm letting you know that I'll need to try and sublet the apartment."

"That's fine. If you can find someone to sublet, then you're no longer obligated. Good luck on finding someone to sublet. Keep me informed."

"I will."

"Goodbye."

"Goodbye."

Immediately, I began asking friends and neighbors if they knew of anyone who'd be interested in renting our apartment. I took out ads in the local newspaper and placed flyers in local businesses. Much to my surprise, I started getting responses almost immediately. Within a few days, a family of three called me up to make an appointment for a tour. They told me that they'd been making plans to move into our community for quite some time, but there had been very few vacancies. So, they were delighted when they saw the ad in the local newspaper. Mr. and Mrs. Jeffries and their young daughter arrived at our apartment at 6:30 PM the following evening. I let them walk through and tour on their own.

Mr. Jeffries said, "This is a beautiful apartment. It has all of the amenities we're looking for. It's close to the lake, close to shopping, and best of all, it's close to our daughter's school."

Mrs. Jeffries asked, "Who do we talk to about signing a lease?"

"You'd talk to the landlord, Mr. Hobbs. But I'll tell you what, let me give him a call and let him know that you're interested. May I have your telephone number so that I can pass it on to him?"

"You sure can. And when will it be available?"

"We'll be moving out at the end of August."

"That's perfect."

"Thank you very much Stephanie. And good luck with your relocation."

"Thank you."

"I'll have Mr. Hobbs contact you."

"Thank you. And thank you for your time."

"You're welcome."

"Good-bye."

"Good-bye."

◆   ◆   ◆

I hoped that everything would work out for the Jeffries family and that they'd be successful in securing a lease and getting the apartment. I also hoped that they would be as happy in their new home as we'd been. It *was* a fabulous apartment. It was in a beautiful brownstone building with a well-manicured courtyard on a gorgeous, tree-lined street. It measured 1,500 square feet at a cost of $600 a month. It had beautiful hardwood floors, two bedrooms, a bathroom, a large, modern eat-in kitchen, a living room, a sunroom with bay windows and a wood-burning fireplace.

I now had to turn my attention to selling my car. Although my car was in mint condition and was extremely dependable, it wasn't exactly a hot commodity. I couldn't imagine that there'd be much interest in a 1986 4-door Chevy Celebrity. But I told my neighbor, Mr. Nichols about it anyway. I figured he might know of someone who could use a nice, dependable car. He surprised me. Right on the spot, he offered to buy it for his son! I thought to myself, "Wow, I must be living right. Everything is just falling right into place."

◆   ◆   ◆

The following week I received a telephone from Mr. Hobbs.

"Stephanie, I wanted you to know that the Jeffries family have signed a lease and will be moving into the apartment on 1 September."

"I'm happy to hear that, Mr. Hobbs."

"Can you tell me the exact date that you'll be vacating?"

"We'll be leaving for the airport on 22 August."

"Well, good luck to you and Christopher. And Stephanie, let me take this opportunity to say thank you for being such a good tenant for all these years.

"Thank you, Mr. Hobbs."

"And when you return to Chicago, stop by to say hello."

"I'll do just that."

Now all I had to do was get passport photos, passports, apply for an international driver's license and then sell or donate all our furniture and other household items.

◆   ◆   ◆

For the first time, it was all beginning to feel real. I was beginning to get excited and was actually beginning to look forward to what lay ahead. I was beginning to experience a new heightened sense of awareness, a new freedom, and a new peace. I was ready to let go of all that was familiar; all that was safe and all that was comfortable and start over all again—fresh and new. For the first time in my life, I was following a dream, going out on a limb and plunging headfirst into the unknown. The thought of it gave me a new sense of self—a fresh surge of energy—and as a result, my enthusiasm soared!

5

Our family, friends, neighbors and co-workers went out of their way to express their love and appreciation by honoring us with a whole host of going away parties. The parties were great, however, by the end of the day on 21 August, I absolutely exhausted. I'd been in perpetual motion since April, and although I was excited, I was beginning to suffer from fatigue. I was actually looking forward to boarding the plane, just so I could get some sleep!

When I went to bed that night, I could barely keep my eyes open; but I couldn't sleep either. I tossed and turned all night. I was either too tired, too excited (or maybe it was a combination of the two) to sleep. Plus, all of our furniture was gone, so it didn't help that we had to sleep on sleeping bags that night. By the time my alarm went off at 4:00 AM., I'd slept all of two hours. I jumped in the shower and then got dressed before I woke Christopher. We had to hurry because my friend, Ben was scheduled to pick us up at 5:00.

By 4:45 AM, our bags were packed, and Christopher and I were sitting on the floor of our vacant apartment, eating bananas and granola bars waiting for my friend Ben to drive us to O'Hare Airport.

◆　　　◆　　　◆

Ben and I had known each other since high school and had become very close. We were actually more like siblings than friends. However, after graduating from high school, we went off to different colleges and lost contact with each other. To save money, I'd enrolled at a local community college with the intention of transferring to a major university after two years. Loyola University of Chicago was my school of choice. I visited the university to register for classes in the summer of 1972. As I was leaving the campus, I heard someone call my name.

"Stephanie."

I said to myself, "Who knows me here?" I turned around.

"Oh my gosh, Ben! What are you doing here?"

"I go to school here. What are *you* doing here?"

"I just enrolled here."

We exchanged telephone numbers and just picked up right where we'd left off two years earlier.

Ben was such a great guy and a trusted friend. He was always the one person I could count on for anything. I'd only hoped that I'd been as good of a friend to him as he'd always been to me.

Ben also had a reputation for being prompt. That's why I was panic-stricken when he was late getting to the apartment.

We were scheduled for an 8:00 AM flight out of O'Hare to LAX which means we needed to leave our apartment by 5:00 (no later than 5:30) But on this day (of all days), Ben was late. And not only was he late, he was *very* late. After the first few minutes I was just surprised, but then I started to worry. I wondered if something could have happened. Between worrying about Ben and worrying about missing our flight, it was more than I could bear. Everything had gone so smoothly up that point, suddenly, I was beside myself with worry. I said to myself, "This can't be happening." I couldn't call him because my telephone had been disconnected. And (as much as I was tempted to) I didn't have the audacity to knock on my neighbor's door at 5:30 in the morning to ask if I could use her telephone. So, all I could do was wait; anxiously wait and pray for Ben's safety.

I started pacing the floor, back and forth, biting my nails, looking out the window every five minutes, and glancing at my watch every three. My palms were beginning to sweat, and my heart was racing "a mile a minute." Five-thirty came and went. Six o'clock came and went. And then at 6:30, Ben came running up the stairs, out of breath and apologizing profusely.

"Steph, I'm so sorry. I ran into a major accident on the expressway and traffic was a bear. I wanted to call you, but I knew your phone was disconnected. Please forgive me."

"Please forgive you? I'm so glad that you're safe."

I grabbed him and gave him the biggest hug, and then I just started to cry. I was so relieved.

"Of course I forgive you. I'm just so glad that you made it here in one piece and that you're safe. I figured something must have gone wrong because you're never late."

"I knew you were depending on me. I hate to disappoint you."

"Don't worry about it. Your safety is more important to me than making a flight. They'll always be another flight. I was less worried about getting to Japan and more worried about you."

By the time we got our luggage, went downstairs and loaded everything into the car, it was 7:00. We lived at least two hours south of the airport, so even with light traffic; I knew we'd miss our flight, but at that point, that didn't much matter. At that point, I could care less about catching a flight. I was just happy to know that my friend was OK.

"Steph, I know you'll miss your scheduled flight, but hopefully you can take a later flight and still make your connection at LAX.

"Ben, I'm not worried about it. I'm sure we'll get to Japan at some point today. Just relax and take your time. It'll all work out."

"Thank you Steph."

"No, thank *you* Ben."

We made it to the airport much behind schedule, but I was just happy that everyone was safe.

"Ben, I appreciate you for offering to drive us to the airport so early in the morning. I'll talk to you when we land at LAX and then we'll talk again when we arrive in Japan."

"I look forward to hearing from you."

"Just take a deep breath and relax my friend. Take your time and make sure you drive safely back to the south side."

"Don't worry I will."

"Take care of yourself. We'll talk soon."

"Have a safe flight."

"We will."

◆   ◆   ◆

Of course, Christopher and I missed our scheduled flight, but we were still able to connect in time for a flight to LAX. We'd arrived late to the airport, but as it turned out, it wasn't so bad after all. And the good thing—it shortened our layover in Los Angeles.

PART II
Life in Japan
(Nihon deno Seikatsu)

o o o o o o o o o o o o o o o o o o o o o o o o o o o o o o o o o o o
"The nail that stands out will be hammered down."

—Japanese Proverb
www.quoteland.com

6

I didn't realize just how grueling international travel could be—especially with a young child in tow. Our flight from Chicago to Los Angeles was five hours long (with a two-hour layover in Los Angeles.) But the longest leg of the trip was yet to come. Little did I know that when we boarded the plane at LAX en route to Seoul, South Korea, that we'd be in the air for 11 hours straight! I wasn't prepared for that—neither was Christopher. Once we landed in Seoul, we had to endure yet another three hour layover. After all that, a one and a half hour flight to Nagoya seemed like "a piece of cake." When we finally arrived in Japan, we'd been traveling for almost 24 hours (and we still had a one hour car trip to Yokkaichi.)

◆　　◆　　◆

After being in the air for eight hours, I was feeling nauseous and very uncomfortable. It was at point I realized that I'd been so focused on all the major things about our trip, that I'd forgotten to inquire about the simple things; things like how to dress comfortably for a long flight (my clothes were much too constrictive) and whether or not I should have brought food for Christopher. I never thought that he wouldn't eat the airplane food. He complained of tummy aches, headaches and he cried incessantly. But the flight attendants were wonderful. They played games with him, brought him special snacks and (when the seat belt sign was turned off) allowed him to get out of his seat and walk around. However, the complaints of tummy aches and headaches persisted. I said to myself, "this is not a good trip." I prayed that he'd sleep, so that I too could get some sleep.

When we boarded the plane in Seoul en route for Nagoya, I knew we only had a little over an hour to go. When the captain made the announcement, "Please take your seats and fasten your seatbelts. We'll be approaching Nagoya International Airport in 15 minutes." Those words were like music to my ears. I felt I could finally exhale when I looked out my window and saw Nagoya's stunning skyline. But I couldn't wait to reach my final destination so I could sleep!

I thought, "Wow, we're finally here. This is wonderful!" But as excited as I was, all I could think about was sleep.

We disembarked and filed through to customs. We approached the customs agent who was very pleasant (and I thought a rather tall) young man. He looked at me and smiled, then at Christopher.

"Do you speak English," he asked.

"Yes, I do."

"May I see your passports please?"

"Yes, here they are."

"What is your business in Japan?"

"I'm here to teach English."

"Ah, Sensei. Welcome to Japan."

"Thank you. Thank you very much."

I said to myself, "Sensei—that sounds very nice. I wonder what it means."

He stamped our passports with the date and a Japanese seal. We claimed our luggage and headed for the exit to meet Kanako. I looked at our surroundings and breathed a sigh of relief, "We're finally here." But in an instant I thought, "Oh my gosh, how will I remember Kanako. I'd only met her once and that had been several months before." But then I thought, "I may not remember how *she* looks, but I'm sure it won't be hard to spot Christopher and I in a Japanese airport. I was right. As we walked through the exit, she spotted us right away.

"Welcome to Japan."

"I'm so happy to finally be here."

"How was your flight?"

"It was a good, but very long and even more exhausting."

"I know. It's not easy."

"Like I said, I'm happy to be here, but I can't wait to freshen up and get some sleep."

"I'll get you to a shower and a bed as fast as I can."

"Wait here while I go and get the car."

We loaded our bags into the trunk of her car and headed south to Yokkaichi!

7

As we exited the airport, it was obvious we weren't in Chicago anymore; everything looked so different—the people, the cars, the houses, the street signs. As we drove south out of Nagoya toward Yokkaichi (pronounced *Yo-kie-chee*), I looked out my window and was in awe as I caught sight of the most beautiful, snow-capped mountainous terrain that I'd ever seen. And at that moment, I realized, having grown up in a prairie state in the mid-west, I'd never seen mountains before (except for in books or at the movies.) Wildflowers and fragrant sakura trees lined the roadsides—it was like a visual feast! Kanako told us that Yokkaichi was about an hour away. Yokkaichi is a beautiful seaside city and the largest in Mie (pronounced *Mee-yeh*) Prefecture with a population of approximately 300,000. Its capital city is Tsu (pronounced *Soo*.)

Kanako asked, "Are you happy to finally be here?"

"I'm thrilled. It seems like we've been traveling forever, but I'm really excited."

"I'm glad to know that. I've told everyone that you and Christopher are coming and they're all anxiously awaiting your arrival."

"That makes me happy. Knowing that everyone's really looking forward to meeting us makes me feel a little less anxious."

"Oh Stephanie, you need not worry. The people of Yoko Dai (pronounced *Die*) and the people of Japan will be very gracious and very accommodating to you and Christopher. Trust me."

"Thank you Kanako, that's so good to hear."

"But also know that you should be prepared to accept gifts from the people you'll meet. It's Japanese tradition to give welcome gifts and to give farewell gifts. You'll receive everything from slippers to Japanese sweets to little trinkets."

"Then I suppose I should learn how to say thank you in Japanese."

"Thank you is *ari-gato* or *ari-gato go-zie-masu* for thank you very much."

"Kanako, I noticed that when we went through customs, the agent asked what my business was in Japan. When I told him I was here to teach, he referred to me as sensei. What does sensei mean?"

"Sensei is teacher and in Japan, sensei is one of the highest honors that can be bestowed upon someone."

"That's nice. I feel honored already!"

◆   ◆   ◆

Kanako said that traffic was unusually light. As a result, we reached Yoko Dai in less than hour. As we approached our community, I looked to my right and caught sight of another set of mountains.

"Kanako, What do you call those mountains?"

"Those are the Goziesho (pronounced *Go-zie-ee-show*) Mountains.

"What direction is that?"

"That's west."

"I'm just trying to get a sense of direction."

Just as we turned left, she pointed to a modern two-story apartment building with four units.

"That's the building where you and Christopher will live."

"Wow! It's very nice. I like it a lot."

"The former tenant has just moved out, so it's not quite move-in ready—it's still being cleaned and painted. However, it should be ready within a couple of days.

"Where will Christopher and I live in the interim?"

"You'll stay at our home. Is that OK with you?"

"That's fine. I just hope that we won't be an imposition to you and your family."

"You won't be; not at all. We're happy to have you."

As we approached Kanako's home, I was struck by its size and beauty.

"Kanako, your home is absolutely beautiful."

"Thank you, Stephanie. We're very proud of it."

"I can see why."

We parked in front of the house, unloaded our luggage and entered through the school on the lower level. As she opened the door, Christopher saw that she removed her shoes before entering. Without being told, he removed his shoes also. (This was his first introduction to Japanese culture.) I removed my shoes and put down my bags.

Sam and Yumi greeted us.

"You finally made it. Welcome to Japan and welcome to our home. It's so nice to meet you. I'm Sam and this is our daughter Yumi."

"It's so nice to meet both of you. We're so happy to be here. And your house; it's absolutely gorgeous."

"Thank you. We enjoy it."

"I can see why."

The Winston house was a large, two-story American-style home that sat on a small mound in the center of the community. Built in the 1980's by an American architect, it was unique in its design and quite a bit larger than the more traditional Japanese homes that surrounded it. It was approximately 3,000 square feet and was large enough to comfortably accommodate the Winston family on the upper level and the Montessori International Language School on the lower level. The family residence had a large living room with a wood-burning fireplace, a dining room that looked out on a wood deck, a spacious, modern kitchen, two bedrooms, a bathroom and a laundry room.

I finally said, "I hate to be rude, but would you mind if I excuse myself and take a shower?"

"We don't mind at all. As a matter of fact, we understand how you need to unwind after such a long flight. This is where you and Christopher will sleep, and this is your bathroom. Let us know if you'll need anything. Take a shower and relax yourself. We'll see you in the morning."

"Thank you, Kanako."

After I showered, I put on my pajamas and went straight to bed. I was asleep by the time my head hit the pillow. I slept through the night, through the morning, and on into the next afternoon. I was finally awakened from what felt like a "Rip Van Winkle" state of sleep, by a knock at the door.

"Stephanie, I know you're really tired and suffering from jet lag, but you can't sleep forever. You have to wake up now."

"Do I have to?"

"Yes my friend, you have to. Don't worry; your body will adjust to the new time zone within a few days."

"Where's Christopher?"

"He's outside at the playground."

"So, he's playing already. That's good."

I showered, got dressed and then had something to eat. It was obvious that Christopher hadn't suffered from jetlag the way I had. He'd been up for hours, had showered, had something to eat and was out playing with a few of the neighborhood children. Two of the three children he'd met were siblings (a boy and a girl) and the third child was a little girl who lived directly across the street from Kanako's home. All the children attended Kanako's school for English language lessons.

Aya and Shin were siblings. They lived with their parents in a neighboring community. Aya was a very beautiful little girl with smooth, olive skin, and almond-shaped eyes. She had short dark brown hair that was cut in a very short bob with bangs. She and Christopher were the same age. Aya was very shy and rarely gave eye contact when she spoke to you or when you spoke to her. She was slow to smile and was very quiet. Her brother Shin was a couple of years younger. He had a beautiful wide smile, a round little face and a short, spiky haircut. He, on the other hand, wasn't shy at all. He smiled and laughed a lot and had no problem looking directly at you when he spoke to you or when you spoke to him. He had a great sense of humor and boundless energy. He was a very funny boy. I liked him right away. The third child was a little girl named Mei. She and Christopher were also the same age. Mei had long, light brown hair, olive skin and beautiful brown eyes. Mei was also quite energetic and was extremely outgoing. She had a younger brother and an older sister. Since the age three, Christopher had always told me how much he hated girls, but for some reason, he seemed to love Mei. She would eventually become his best *girl* friend.

For the first few days of our arrival, Christopher didn't have much of a routine. He seemed pretty happy and carefree. He slept as late as he wanted, woke up, had something to eat and then went outside to play. For the first time in his life, there were no demands placed upon him; no expectations and little to no structure. But little did he know; that was about to change. Little did he know that reality was about to set in.

◆   ◆   ◆

The following day, we were all up bright and early. Kanako said, "Stephanie, I'd like to take you and Christopher to meet my grandmother, my parents and my sister and her family."

"That would be great. Do they live far from here?"

"No. Not at all. As a matter of fact, they live in my childhood home which is actually quite close."

We drove about half a mile to Kanako's family home. It was a beautiful, large, traditional Japanese house. As we approached the entrance with its well-manicured landscape complete with flowering plants, bonsai trees, the sounds of trickling water and the sight of carp (*koi*) friskily swimming in the pond, it immediately put me in a tranquil, peaceful mood.

We entered the home and removed our shoes. All the family members graciously met us at the door. Everyone seemed happy to see us. Kanako's mother, Kawayama-san made us welcomed by offering us Japanese tea and sweets. We graciously accepted. Kanako's father took an immediate liking to Christopher.

He left the room and returned with a box of toys for him to play with, which immediately endeared him to Christopher. Kawayama-san would eventually become the grandfather that Christopher never had!

8

Just as Kanako had told me, the jetlag did fade away and my body and brain did indeed begin to adjust to the new time zone. I was now ready to take on Yokkai-chi!

"Kanako, do you think you could drive me to the bank to have my dollars converted to yen?"

"I'd love to drive you. Actually you're in luck."

"Why so?"

"Because the exchange rate is very good right now—$1 equals about 124 yen."

"That *is* very good. That means my dollar will go much further here. Wow, I guess I am pretty lucky."

"After I drive you to the bank, would you like to take a trip to the grocer?"

"I think that would be great. I need to start getting a feel for the neighborhood anyway."

"Well, we have several local stores, but I'll drive you to *Ichi-go-Kan* Grocery Store because it's closest to us; as a matter of fact, it's within walking distance of your apartment."

"Seeing that I don't have a car here, it's good to know that we have a store that's within walking distance."

Before I left Chicago for Japan, I purchased an English/Japanese Dictionary. And every time I stepped foot outside of Kanako's home, I made sure I took along a pencil, paper and my trusty dictionary. I was constantly asking Kanako, "How do you say *this;* how do you say *that*?"

For example, I needed to know how to ask, "How much is this please?" *("I-kura desuka kudasai?")* Or, "Where is the bank please?" *("Ginko doko desuka, kudasai?")* Or, "May I have a drink of water please?" *("Mizu kudasai.")*

I knew that Christopher and I would be on our own within a matter of days, and although Kanako would still be available to help us, I wanted to acquire as much information as I possibly could so that I could start to reclaim my independence.

◆   ◆   ◆

After three days, our apartment was ready.

"So, Stephanie, are you ready to see your new apartment?"

"I'm *so* ready."

"Before you see it, I need to forewarn you; it's quite small, especially compared to your apartment in Chicago."

"Don't worry. I can't imagine that our apartment here would be anything like our apartment in Chicago. I'd expect it to be smaller."

"I just don't want you to have any unrealistic expectations and be disappointed."

"I'm in Japan. I'm excited. There's no way I'm going to be disappointed."

Our apartment was within walking distance of Kanako's home. It was on the second floor.

As we opened the door and walked in, I was struck by its brightness and pristine beauty. It was indeed small, but not quite as small as I'd expected. It measured about 600 square feet. I said to myself, "This will truly be a lesson in "learning to live with less."

◆   ◆   ◆

Directly behind the front door was a built-in cabinet with sliding doors. To the left of the door was a rice carpet (*tatami*) room with sliding doors and to the right a small laundry room that was just large enough to house a small washing machine, but no dryer. (Most families in Yoko Dai didn't own dryers; they'd wash their clothes and then hang them outside on clotheslines to dry.) The laundry room also had a sink with a mirror/medicine cabinet just above it. Next to the laundry/sink room was a small room that housed a shower and a bathtub (*ofuro*). In Japan, families shower prior to bathing. The bathtub is for soaking only. Everyone soaks in the same bath in order to conserve water. (Eventually, Christopher and I would conform to the same practice.) Families also showered at night before going to bed. A few steps down the hall on the right was a small room with a "western-style" commode. And a few steps from there was a small kitchen with an eat-in area. Just off the kitchen was our living room. The kitchen and living room had a wall of sliding glass doors that lead outside to a small patio. Our kitchen faced east toward the rice fields and our front faced west toward Go-zie-sho Mountains.

Due to space constraints in Japan, most of the rooms in homes and apartment houses serve multiple functions. Our (*tatami*) room served as my bedroom and my office, and the living area served as Christopher's bedroom, his play room and as our dining room.

"So, Stephanie, what do you think?"

"It's small alright, but I like it. It's so bright and cheery. I'm really looking forward to fixing it up and making it ours."

"Can you believe this is the size of the average apartment in Japan?"

"Is that so?"

"Yes. And, it's not unusual for a family of four to occupy a space this size."

"So, I guess this would be considered large for only two people huh?"

"You're absolutely right."

"Then I guess we're lucky. How much is rent?"

"Rent is $600 a month."

"That's the same amount I paid for our apartment in Chicago."

"You'll be paying the same money, but you'll be getting much less space."

"That's OK, I'm sure we'll get used to it."

"I just hope you'll enjoy living here."

"I know we will. I'm actually looking forward to it."

"So what would you like to do now?"

"I'd love to go shopping for some furniture so I can start fixing it up. Do you think you can take me?"

"I'd love to take you, but before we go, would you mind if I contact a couple of my friends to see if they can loan you some things so that you don't have to purchase everything?"

"I don't mind at all."

"That's good, because I know that the plan is for you to only stay for one year, so you don't want to spend money on items that you'll just end up leaving behind."

"You're absolutely right."

"I'll contact some of the neighbors, to see what they can help out with, and then, we'll go shopping tomorrow. Does that sound good?"

"That sounds great."

"Meanwhile, do you mind staying at our house for one more night?"

"I don't mind at all."

◆ ◆ ◆

Amidst the excitement and the anticipation of shopping for new furniture to fix up our new apartment, I had no problem waking up bright and early the following morning. We had breakfast and left home at 9:00 AM. I purchased some items I needed right away—a child-size futon for Christopher, an adult-size futon for myself, a small refrigerator, a low table for eating (*kotatsu*) and a washing machine. The neighbors loaned us a sofa, a table and four chairs for the kitchen and a rice cooker. Over time, I purchased dishes, flatware, towels and other items to help personalize the space. The following day, we moved in.

9

For several months leading up to our department, I'd been caught up in a virtual whirlwind of excitement. And as a result, I'd never taken the time to pause for long enough to really think about how this adventure might affect Christopher (or myself for that matter.)

Since Christopher and I had arrived in Yokkaichi, we'd been the center of attention; much like "the belle and beau of the ball." Since the day we first arrived, we'd been completely overjoyed and overwhelmed by the warm and welcoming reception we'd received. We'd been showered with gifts and we were once again honored guests at a whole host of parties and celebrations. Up to this point, it had been all fun and games. Life was simple; it was easy—especially for Christopher. Up to this point, he'd done little else except play, eat, drink and attend parties. In his mind, coming to Japan was like one big party; one big vacation. He'd soon realize that wasn't the case at all.

◆　　　◆　　　◆

Culture shock is defined as the anxiety that people experience as they encounter and try to adapt to the customs and expectations of another culture.

◆　　　◆　　　◆

Food—it's our life source. We all need it. We all love it. We find solace in it. We celebrate with it. We mourn with it. We eat when we're happy; we eat when we're sad. We give it as a reward for good behavior, and we deprive it as a form of punishment. It brings us comfort; it brings us joy.

I'd never realized just how much eating and feeding are reflected in people's culture, in their histories and in their relationships. Eating can be a happy, celebratory time, full of joy and laughter or it can be a fearful time, full of anxiety and avoidance.

In Japan, like in many cultures, gathering around the family table is tradition. In Japan, every meal is an event and a chance to connect with family and friends.

One of the best ways to define a people and their culture is through their language, their music, but mostly, it's through their food. In the past, I'd never given much thought to the culture or the tradition of food, and I had never really understood its importance—until now.

When we first traveled to Japan, I anticipated a language barrier; I anticipated culture shock, but I never dreamed that there'd be issues involving food. Language barriers are real, culture shock is real, and food barriers are also real. I soon found out just *how* real.

◆　　　◆　　　◆

For Christopher, his first exposure to culture shock came in the form of food. The foods were foreign in appearance and in aroma. He wasn't about to sample foods he couldn't even pronounce. He'd always been a finicky eater, but now he was really being challenged. In Japan, rice (*go-han*) is the staple food. However, bread *(pan)* has also become quite popular and tea (*o-cha*) the predominant drink. For weeks on end, Christopher ate only bread and rice. I was deeply concerned because he wasn't eating fruit, vegetables, meat, chicken or fish. I'd tried to no avail to get more variety into his diet. I was at my wits end, so I called Kanako.

"Kanako, I'm really concerned about Christopher."

"Why so?"

"He's only eating bread and rice. I can't get him to try anything else, not even an apple or an orange."

"Don't worry. It's perfectly normal for a child who travels to a foreign country to have no interest in sampling the local foods. Believe me, he'll start sampling a wider variety of foods and will slowly begin to acquire a taste for them. As long as he's eating *something,* he won't starve. I know it's hard for you so see him eating only rice and bread, but in time, he'll want more."

I trusted Kanako. So, as hard it was for me, I tried to take her advice and calm down.

10

On one of our trips to the grocer, a child pointed at me and said, *"Gai-jin."* The child's mother looked mortified. She looked at me, bowed and said, *"Gomen na-sai."* I wasn't offended, by the word *"Gai-jin,"* but I *was* curious as to what it meant. When I returned home I called Kanako.

"Kanako, today as we walked to the grocer, a child pointed at me and said *"gai-jin."* What is *"gai-jin?"*

"Gai-jin" is foreigner."

"Oh is that it?"

"That's it."

"What does *gomen na-sai* mean?"

"That means I'm sorry."

"That's what the child's mother said to me. I guess she was embarrassed and felt the need to apologize for her child's outburst."

"The child's reaction, although inappropriate, it was indeed understandable."

"Why do you say that?"

"It's because Japan is one of the most homogenous societies in the world. Most Japanese have the same expectations, share the same language, have the same culture and for the most part, have similar lifestyles. In the larger cities like Tokyo, Nagoya or Yokohama, there are varying degrees of diversity due to the influx of foreign nationals who live, work or attend the universities there, but here in Yokkaichi (and namely, here in Yoko Dai) that's not the case. Many people, mostly the very old or the very young haven't had much exposure to foreigners. For them, it's surprising to see a non-Japanese person."

"Kanako, do you remember our first meeting back in Chicago?"

"Of course I do. I'll never forget it."

"Well you do remember that I had some reservations and some serious concerns about race relations here in Japan. I didn't know what to expect, and of course I feared the worse."

"Yes, and I remember that I told you that you and Christopher had nothing to worry about. And you know what; you still don't have anything to worry about."

"I'm actually starting to believe that now. We've met some wonderful people who've been more than kind to us. We haven't encountered any problems."

"But Stephanie, there is one thing you and Christopher should be aware of."

"What's that?"

"You may notice that sometimes the Japanese have a tendency to stare; especially at foreigners."

"Why do they stare?"

"I think the staring can come off as being a sign of rudeness, but that's not the case at. It's just that many people are fascinated by foreigners, especially those who've not had much exposure to them."

"That's good to know. I'm glad you're telling me."

"I'm telling you because I don't want you or Christopher to take it personally.

"Kanako, now that we're on the subject of race and ethnicity, I have something else I'd like to share with you."

"What is it?"

"I've noticed that since Christopher and I have been here in Japan, race and ethnicity really doesn't seem to be an issue. Everyone refers to us as *American* as opposed to *Black American* or *African-American*. I have to tell you, it's the first time in my life that I've been described by my *nationality* and not by my *ethnicity*."

"That's great."

"Tell me, what do you think about that?"

"I love it. I find it to be quite refreshing."

"How is what you're experiencing here, different from what you're experiencing in the U.S.?"

"In the U.S. I'm African *first* and American *second*.

"That's interesting. How do you feel about that?"

"Well, it's not that I'm not proud of who I am, it's just that people tend to focus on the things that make us different as opposed to the things that make us the same. And for those of us who were born in America, we *are* more alike than we're different. We speak the same language, we all love our children, and for the most part, we all have the same goals and the same aspirations."

"I'm glad you can appreciate the fact that the Japanese view you and Christopher as *Americans*. And I'm also glad that you feel that the people of Japan have welcomed you and Christopher with open arms.

"I do. I really do. And I'm enjoying it."

"That's great."

11

The day of reckoning was finally upon us. The time had come to get Christopher registered at school.

◆　　◆　　◆

Prior to our arrival, Kanako had visited the local public school—Tokiwanishi School *(Tokiwanishi Sho Gakko)* and met with the principal *(ko-jo sensei)* to talk about Christopher.

"Kojo-Sensei, I have hired an American teacher to work in my school next year. She has a six year-old son named Christopher who'll be in first grade. I know that in the history of Tokiwanishi, the school has never enrolled a non-Japanese child."

"Yes, that's true. We've never enrolled a child outside of the area."

"Would you be willing to make an exception and accept Christopher? And do you think you can accommodate him?"

"Yes, to both questions. We would gladly accept him, and we'll try our best to accommodate him. We don't really have the supports, but we are definitely willing to try."

"I'm happy to know that."

"When are he and his mother scheduled to arrive?"

"They'll arrive at the end of August."

"School will already be in session at that time, but I'm sure we can work something out."

"Is there a particular teacher you have in mind; one who you think can work with him?"

"As a matter of fact I do. We have a very fine first grade teacher. She's young and enthusiastic, and she has lots of energy. Her name's Nori Mika."

"Thank you, Ko-jo sensei. I'm thrilled to know that you and your staff are willing to work with Christopher. I'm sure his mother will be happy as well. And when they arrive in August we'll visit the school and get Christopher enrolled.

"We look forward to seeing you again."

"Goodbye."

"Goodbye."

◆   ◆   ◆

The night before we were scheduled to visit Tokiwanishi school, I sat down with Christopher to share the news with him.

"Christopher, I want you to know that Kanako and I will drive you to your new school tomorrow so you can meet your principal and your new teacher. How does that sound?"

"That sound good mommy."

"Are you excited?"

"Yes. I can hardly wait to see my new school."

"That's good Christopher. I'm looking forward to it also."

"Let's make sure we get to bed on time so we can be up bright and early."

◆   ◆   ◆

Tokiwanishi School was a stone's throw away from Kanako's home and an equal distance from our apartment. She drove Christopher and me for our interview to enroll him and meet his new teacher *(sensei)* and his principal *(kojo-sensei.)*

We arrived at the school at 9 AM; walked through the main entrance; removed our outdoor shoes and replaced them with the indoor slippers that were provided. We walked past the main office and down the long hallway to Mr. Yamaguchi's office. Mr. Yamaguchi was a short, middle-aged gentleman. He had a very pleasant face, silver-gray hair and he wore black horn-rimmed glasses. He was immaculately dressed in a brown suit, with a white shirt and a brown and black tie. When we approached his office and knocked at the door, he was seated at his desk and talking with Nori sensei. When they spotted us at the entrance, each stood up, greeted us with bow, shook my hand and then turned to Christopher and shook his hand. Nori-san was quite young and quite small in stature. When she stood up, she wasn't much taller than Christopher. Her skin was smooth and flawless and she wore her black hair in a very short pixie cut.

"Hello, Chris-kun. I'm Nori Mika. I'm your new sensei." (In Japan, *"kun"* is a term of endearment used for young boys. For example, Chris-kun, Kenji-kun or Taki-kun. *"Chan"* is the term used for young girls. For example, Mari-chan, Miki-chan or Mei-chan.) She knelt down and took his face in both her hands and smiled at him. It soon became obvious that her English was very limited. I thought to myself, "This is not going to be easy; for Christopher or for me." I asked myself, "How's he going to manage in a classroom where he can't speak Japanese and his teacher can't speak English?"

Although everyone seemed very kind and it was obvious that they were all trying to make an effort to make Christopher feel welcomed, I still felt uneasy due to our inability to communicate. I wondered if Tokiwanishi would be able to accommodate him and if the faculty was equipped to meet his needs. I thought, "If they can't talk to him then how in the world are they going to be able to work with him?"

Nori-san turned to Kanako and handed her a piece of paper. She said it was a list of supplies that Christopher would need for his first day. As a show of respect, Kanako gave the list to me (even though she knew I couldn't read it.)

We said goodbye and left the building.

"Kanako, that was a very pleasant, but a very stressful meeting."

"I can understand your frustration. But don't worry. Things will work out for you and for Christopher."

"I can appreciate your enthusiasm and your optimism, but I'm still very nervous."

"I know you are. That's perfectly understandable. But things will work out. Trust me."

"Can you tell me what this school list says and can we go shopping for the supplies?"

"We sure can. Let's go right now."

"When will Christopher start school?"

"He'll start tomorrow.

"Wow, so soon?"

"The sooner he gets started, the sooner he can start developing a routine and the better it'll be for him.

"I agree. He really needs to get back on a schedule."

We drove to the local school supply store and bought a school cap, two school uniforms, indoor shoes, a thermos and other school supplies. The school provided all his textbooks. He had everything he needed—at least I thought he did.

◆   ◆   ◆

Anxiety and frustration became overriding emotions for me. I no longer felt empowered because I'd lost my ability to communicate. I wouldn't be able to talk to his teachers, and I wouldn't be able to ask questions regarding his progress;

and in turn, his teachers wouldn't be able to talk to me. I was totally dependent on Kanako to serve as my translator (and that wasn't easy.) All my life, I'd been such an independent spirit. This was going to take some getting used to. I felt vulnerable. I felt like I'd give up my power; my control, and I didn't like it; I was totally frustrated. All my formal education couldn't serve me now because without the ability to speak a language, one loses the most basic of human needs—the need to connect; the need to communicate. For the first time in my life I felt completely incompetent, inadequate and insecure. I said to myself, "Stephanie, if you want to be in control of your environment and if you want to have the ability to communicate with Christopher's teachers, then you'll definitely need to learn to speak Japanese." I was on a mission to learn.

◆　　　◆　　　◆

As mandated by MONBUSHO, the National Government Education Board, schools in Japan were in session approximately 224 days a year (compared to 180 days for most schools in the United States.) Another striking difference was that classes were also held on the 2nd and 4th Saturdays of the month, from 8:00 AM to 12:00 noon.

In the United States, most schools begin the school year in August or September. In Japan, however, the school year began in April. When Christopher and I arrived in Yokkaichi, in August, school had been in session for four months.

Japanese schools differed from American schools in many other ways. Here are a few of those differences:

- All curriculums were set by MONBUSHO and were standard throughout Japan.

- Students stayed together in the classrooms at the elementary, junior high, and high school levels.

- Students didn't change classes between periods; the teachers changed rooms.

- Students were much more unsupervised. If the teachers had a meeting, they would inform the students and then leave the classroom. The expectation was that the students would discipline themselves and complete assignments.

- There was rarely a substitute. If the teacher was absent, assignments were written on the chalkboard and teachers from neighboring classrooms would periodically look in on the students.

- Children stayed with the same teacher for first (*ichi-nen-sei*) and second (*ni-nin-sei*) grades.

- Tokiwanishi (as was the case at most schools) had no custodial help. The students and teachers were expected to clean and mop all classrooms and hallways.

In Japan, kindergarten was not compulsory. However, most children did attend kindergarten (what we call preschool in the U.S.) for three years. During this time they were taught social skills, reading, and writing. Children officially began school at age six (first grade.) All children carried rugged leather backpacks called *ran-do-seru*. The boys' *ran-do-seru* was typically black, and the girls' either red or pink. The *ran-do-seru* was extremely well made and extremely sturdy. Often, the same *ran-do-seru* would be carried by a student for his or her entire school life (from 1st through 12th grades.) For the first few days of school, Christopher carried his traditional American backpack. Fortunately, I didn't have to purchase one because our neighbor, Nakamoto-san's son had recently graduated from high school, so she loaned Christopher his *ran-do-seru*.

In Japan, the first nine years of school were compulsory; however, the three years of senior high school were not. There were six years of elementary school (1st through 6th grades), three years of junior high school (7th through 9th grades), and three years of senior high school (10th through 12th grades).

◆   ◆   ◆

In 1992, Tokiwanishi School was celebrating its 20th anniversary. Approximately 600 students ranging in age from 6 to 12 years in 1st grade (*ichi-nen-sei*) through 6th grade (*roku-nen-sei*) were enrolled. There were no school buses, so children walked to and from school in small groups. The boys walked in their groups and the girls walked in separate groups. The oldest children (the 6th graders) served as "group leaders." Each morning, they went from house to house and rounded up the younger children. Our apartment was right at the edge of Yoko Dai, so Christopher was the last child to get picked up in the morning and the first child to be dropped off after school. At the end of the day, the group leaders waited for all the children in their group to gather in a specified area, and they all walked home together. For the first few days of school, the leader from Christopher's group would ring our doorbell at 7:15 AM to pick him up. After about a week, Christopher would get dressed, eat breakfast and go downstairs to meet his group.

◆　　　◆　　　◆

On the first day of school, Christopher was up bright and early at 6:45 AM. He put away his futon, groomed himself, ate a breakfast of bread and fruit juice and waited for his group leader to pick him up at 7:15 AM.

The first few of days of school went smoothly and without incident. But of course, I was curious as to how things were going. After a week, I decided to ask.

"Christopher, how was your day?"

"It was OK."

"It was just OK?"

"Yes, Mom, just OK."

I knew he was struggling and I knew he was having a hard time, but he never said anything; he never complained. I also knew he was at a disadvantage and had faced what appeared to be insurmountable challenges from the very first day of school. School had already been in session for four months when he arrived. And I knew that he didn't have any friends yet. He wasn't eating very much and he couldn't speak the language. After a while, he just tuned out altogether.

One afternoon while I was preparing an early dinner, I walked out on the patio to air out our futons by hanging them over the railing. I looked east in the direction of the rice fields and caught sight of a lone little boy in a red cap walking in the direction of our home. I wondered to myself, "why is there a little boy walking by himself? I wonder who he is." I stood there for a while and as he got closer I soon realized that it was Christopher! But I thought, "Why would Christopher be walking home by himself, especially, when school was still in session?" I started to worry. Within minutes, he walked into the apartment.

"Christopher, why are you home so early. Are you sick?"

"No, I'm not sick. I just left."

"What do you mean, you just left?"

"I just stood up, got my backpack, got my jacket, and walked out."

"Why'd you do that?"

"Well, I couldn't understand what sensei was saying, so I just came home."

"Christopher, I know you're frustrated and I know you can't understand your sensei, but honey, you can't just walk out of the classroom. You have to wait until you're officially dismissed. I'll tell you what; let's try again tomorrow, OK?"

"I can't mom. I can't go back. I hate it. I hate school. I hate Japan. And I hate the Japanese. I want to go home. I want to go back to Chicago." He started to cry. I felt miserable. I asked myself, "Stephanie, what have you done? Was it a mistake to bring him here?"

"Christopher, it's not nice to say you hate Japan and that you hate the Japanese. I know you're upset, but don't say "hate," that's a strong word; it's a negative word."

"But I do mom, I hate everything."

"I know this isn't easy for you son, but if you work with me, I promise, it'll get better."

I tried to console him with a big hug and a kiss. We ate a snack together and talked about it. He seemed to calm down.

"Do you feel better?"

"A little bit."

"So, will you try it again tomorrow?"

"Yes. I'll try it again."

"That's my boy."

◆   ◆   ◆

With Christopher settled, I could now focus on my work at the Montessori International Language School. My first few weeks of teaching were almost as stressful and as challenging for me as Christopher's first weeks at school had been for him. I taught several different English sessions. My students ranged in age from preschool to adult and they all had different schedules. The biggest challenge that I faced was in trying schedule classes that could accommodate all of them. Monday through Friday I taught English to 3-6 year olds in a Montessori setting; in the afternoon I taught English language and American culture to elementary-age children; and in the evenings I offered classes to high school students. One morning a week I taught conversational English to young women and two nights a week I tutored Japanese businessmen.

But my favorite class by far, was the conversational class that I taught on Wednesday mornings from 11:00 AM to 12 noon. It was comprised of six women who spoke English with varying degrees of proficiency. Many of them had traveled to Europe, Hawaii or Australia, and some had even lived in the U.S. as nationals. We formed an immediate bond and became fast friends. They often included me in their extracurricular activities. We'd shop, dine and sometimes even travel together. I provided them lessons in English language and American culture; they in turn provided me lessons in Japanese language and Japanese culture.

My grade school and high school students also spoke with varying degrees of English, and many of them had also done some international travel with their families or had traveled to or lived in the U.S. for short periods.

I thoroughly enjoyed my work; however, I found that, more often than not, I struggled with the language, especially when I tried to communicate with the parents of some of my younger students. Oftentimes parents would approach me with a question or a comment about their child, but I'd always have to refer to Kanako for help. I was frustrated and humiliated all the time. I asked Kanako to help me learn different words and phrases so that, even if I couldn't carry on a conversation, at least I could exchange greetings or niceties with parents. And then, as if things weren't bad enough, one of my younger students arrived at school one day, walked up to Kanako and said,

"Kanako sensei, Allen sensei is *buta*." I thought, *"buta,"* that sounds cute; maybe it's a term of endearment.

I asked Kanako, "What does *buta* mean?"

"*Buta* means pig?"

"It means pig. Really?"

"It does. And I apologize that you had to hear that."

"No, no. Don't apologize. It's not your fault."

"Stephanie, most of the children have never seen a tall woman before. You're actually taller than most of their fathers."

"No, I understand." I guess by Japanese standards, I was pretty big and tall. It still didn't make me feel good though. I knew I had to do something about my weight. I figured if the children were *saying* I was fat; then the adults were *thinking* I was fat!

I couldn't get *"buta"* out of my head. I'd never been called fat before. But being referred to as *"buta,"* well now, that was just the incentive I needed to get started on a plan.

◆   ◆   ◆

Several days passed, but Christopher's level of frustration remained high. His frustration began to manifest itself into negative behavior. He began acting out in class and he began hitting and biting his classmates. By no means did I condone his behavior, but I *did* understand it. I knew that he was experiencing a classic case of culture shock. But I thought his teachers might view his negative behavior as a direct reflection on me; on my parenting skills (or lack thereof.) I was dreadfully embarrassed. I was embarrassed because the staff at Tokiwanishi had gone out of their way to accommodate him, and I thought to myself, "And this is how he was repaying them for their kindness?" I felt so guilty because I felt like we'd disappointed them; like we'd let them down. My fear was that he'd be suspended; worse yet, that he'd be expelled.

From the time he was a toddler, I'd always taught Christopher to request what he wanted and to express himself by "using his words." But this time, it was different. This time he couldn't use his words because he *had* no words; that is, no words that could be understood. And that was the problem. His negative behavior had actually *become* his new form of communication. He was indeed communicating; even if ever so negatively. His behavior said that he was angry and that he frustrated (and rightfully so.)

I was constantly on "pins and needles," never knowing when I'd receive a telephone call from the school. And then it happened. One day while in class, the telephone at the Montessori school rang. Kanako answered it. All I could hear her say was, "tomorrow evening at 6:00 PM." When she hung up she said to me,

"Stephanie, that was Yamaguchi-san from Tokiwanishi. He and Nori sensei would like to meet with us to discuss Christopher. They'll be here at 6:00 tomorrow." It was as if my worse nightmare had come true.

Yamaguchi-san, Nori-san, Kanako and I met a Kanako's home the following evening. At the last minute, I decided that Christopher was old enough to be included in our conference. I thought he should be present if we were going to be talking *about* him. I thought his presence might even help to "shed some light" on the subject. As it turned out, Yamaguchi-san said that Christopher's behavior had actually gotten worse. He said he was being defiant, wasn't cooperating and wasn't following directions. He said he had begun screaming and was continuously hitting and kicking the other children. That type of behavior was considered atypical for children in Japan (actually, it was atypical for Christopher too. He'd always been such a sweet, easy-going little boy, who'd never had any disciplinary problems.) But suddenly, his behavior was proving to be particularly challenging for his teachers (and for me too for that matter.) The staff didn't know how to handle him, and their inability to communicate with him, just made matters worse. My hands were tied; I didn't know what I was going to do. I was surprised when Yamaguchi-san said, "I know this is very hard for Chris-kun, but we don't want to give up on him. We understand his behavior to be that of a little boy who is confused and who's struggling to adjust to a new language and a new culture. We want to continue working with him and in time, we think he'll be successful." Yamaguchi-san and Nori-san agreed to give Christopher another chance. And we all hoped that in time, everything would work out.

I said, "Kanako, would you please tell them that I appreciate all their support and their willingness to work with Christopher, and that we will do all that we can to try and help him adjust." Kanako translated my statement. Yamaguchi-san said, "Arigato gozaimasu." ("Thank you very much.")

When Yamaguchi-san and Nori-san left for the evening, I turned to Kanako and said,

"Kanako, what would you think about me enrolling Christopher in a school where English is spoken?"

"Well, that's definitely an option, but the closest English school is in Nagoya. Are you prepared to take him to school every morning by train?"

"No. Not really. That would be impossible. But I'm so frustrated and so is he."

"Do you want him to learn to speak Japanese?"

"I do, but not at any cost."

"If you place him in a school where English is spoken, he'll gravitate toward the language he understands. He'll tune out on all the Japanese and will have no interest in learning to speak; he'll have no need to learn to speak. Trust me. If you take him out of Tokiwanishi, he probably won't learn to speak Japanese. Is that really what you want?"

"No it's not; not really."

"Then I'll tell you what, let's leave him at Tokiwanishi for a while longer and let's see what happens. But in the meantime, if you'd like, I can contact my friend, Osaka-san and ask her if she would be willing to help Christopher out at school. Would you like to try that for a while?" (Osaka-san was one of the ladies from my Wednesday morning class. Osaka-san also served as a substitute teacher at the Montessori school.)

"I'd *love* to try that for a while. Hopefully, it'll help. Thank you, Kanako. I really appreciate your support."

"It's my pleasure. You know that we all want Christopher to succeed just as much as you do."

◆   ◆   ◆

Osaka-san and Kanako had known each other since they were young girls and gone to grade school and high school together. She too had grown up in Yokkaichi and had lived there all of her life. She'd moved to Yokohama for a while, had gotten married and returned to Yokkaichi. She and her husband had been married for 15 years and were the proud parents of two lovely teenage daughters. Kanako called her that same evening.

"Osaka-san, this is Kanako. Christopher is struggling at Tokiwanishi, so I was wondering if you could do me a favor and go to his school two or three days a week to help him with translation."

"I'd love to help Christopher. I'll contact his teacher and make arrangements to go in and help out."

"Thank you Osaka-san."

"You're welcome. We all want to do whatever we can to ensure Christopher's success."

I introduced Christopher to Osaka-san and told him that she would come to his school two or three days a week to work with him and help him to understand what the sensei and the children were saying.

"Would you like that Christopher?"

"Yes, mom, maybe that'll help me."

"I'm sure it will."

◆   ◆   ◆

Osaka-san met Christopher in his classroom the following day. They worked together Mondays, Wednesdays and Fridays. In the beginning, she'd go into his classroom, take him out and work with him one-on-one in a private room. Over time, they became very good friends. The arrangement seemed to be working quite well. Several months passed.

One evening while we were having dinner, Christopher looked up and proudly announced,

"Mom, I don't need Osaka-san anymore."

"What do you mean you don't need Osaka-san anymore?"

"I mean, I don't need her help anymore."

"I think you do Christopher."

"No I don't mom."

"Why do you say you don't need her anymore?"

"Well, when Osaka-san comes in to my classroom to take me out, I feel like I miss more than I would if I just stayed in my room."

I was quite surprised to hear him say that he no longer needed Osaka-san's help and that he felt it would be better for him to remain in his classroom. I took that to mean that he was probably starting to catch on; that he was probably starting to adjust. I took it to mean that he was ready to be a part of the group. In a way, I felt like our mission was being accomplished. This was the first step in the right direction. I was thrilled!

"OK Christopher, if you think you can do this by yourself then I'll call Osaka-san and tell her that you no longer need her help."

"That's fine mom."

When we finished dinner, I called Osaka-san.

"Moshi Moshi, Osaka desu."

"Moshi Moshi, Osaka-san, this is Stephanie."

"Hello, Stephanie-san. How are you?"

"I'm fine. How are you?"

"I'm good."

"First of all, Osaka-san, I wanted to thank you for all you've done for Christopher."

"It's been my pleasure. He's doing extremely well. I'm very proud of him."

"That's the reason for my call. He says he doesn't need your help anymore. I hope you're not offended by that."

"I'm not offended at all. If anything, I'll take it as a compliment. This is what we wanted. We wanted him to reach the point where he didn't need special help anymore. I think it's great that he knows he's ready to try it on his own. It makes me feel like I've done my job."

"Thank you Osaka-san. Thank you for understanding. I don't know what we would have done without you."

"It's been my pleasure. And if you need my help in the future, please don't hesitate to ask me."

"I'll do just that."

"Goodbye."

"Goodbye."

◆   ◆   ◆

Several weeks passed and Christopher and I were well into our daily routine. One evening at dinner, I decided to ask again,

"So, Christopher, how was your day?"

"It was great."

"Oh really? You had a great day?"

"Yes, I had a great day. And you know what else mom?"

"What's that Chris?"

"I'm part *American* and part *Japanese.*"

I thought, "How cute."

"No Chris. You're an American who *lives* in Japan and *speaks* Japanese. You're not *part* Japanese.

"No mom. I really am part American and part Japanese."

He was convinced. I decided not to argue with him. I thought, "Maybe this is a good thing; maybe this means he's starting to adjust; starting to assimilate. I thought to myself, he's young, he'll soon learn the truth. For now, I'm just happy that he's no longer angry or frustrated."

I decided to change the subject.

"So Christopher, tell me, what do you and your friends talk about when you walk to and from school?"

"I don't talk, Mom, I just listen."

"Do you understand what they're saying?"

"I understand a little bit. I can understand *some* of the words, but I don't understand everything they're saying, but I listen anyway."

Listening was good. Maybe if he listened long enough, he might eventually begin to speak. But I was just happy because his behavior had changed; he was no longer hitting, kicking or biting his classmates, and he was no longer saying that he hated Japan or hated the Japanese.

"Christopher, I'm very happy for you and I'm very proud of you."

"Thanks mom."

With each passing day, things seemed to get a little better. But I was still concerned about his diet. At breakfast, he'd slowly begun eating fruits, cereals and eggs, but overall, his diet was still pretty limited. At Tokiwanishi, parents could pay a small fee and have lunch provided for their children or children could opt to bring their own lunch. I chose to pay the fee. But still, I wondered what he was eating for lunch. So I asked him,

"Christopher, how's the lunch at school and what do you eat?"

"I don't like the food mom, so I just drink the juice."

"You mean you don't eat anything?"

"Sometimes I eat the rice or the bread."

I was in a panic. That meant he wasn't eating anything between breakfast and an afternoon snack at 2:30 or 3:00! I decided to pack him a lunch. I bought a lunch box and packed it with foods I knew he would eat—a tuna sandwich, a tossed salad, fresh fruit and cookies. And, even if he didn't eat everything, I felt much better in knowing that at least there was *something* in his box that he liked.

12

From the moment Christopher began consuming a larger quantity and a wider variety of foods, everything about him seemed to change—his disposition; his posture; his attitude. He even seemed to gain a couple of pounds (which he desperately needed.) Seeing the changes that were slowly taking place in him, only made me feel better; it made my life easier.

And then, the day I'd been waiting for finally arrived. I was in the kitchen (as I often was) preparing an early dinner when he came charging up the stairs of our apartment building, flung open the door, threw down his *ran-do-seru* and said,

"Mom, I'm going outside to play with my *tomodachi*."

"Your *tomodachi*, what does that mean?"

"*Tomodachi* means friend, mom. I'm going to play with my friend, Nobu."

"Where will you be?"

"We're going to the playground."

"Would you like your snack?"

"I'll have it later. I have to go."

"OK, well, have fun."

"I will. Bye."

"Bye."

Christopher's new friend was Nobu Watanabe. Nobu lived with his mother and father and two brothers in a beautiful, large, traditional Japanese home, directly across the street and just north of our apartment building. I'd seen Nobu walking to and from school with Christopher on numerous occasions, but I had no idea that they'd become such good friends. Nobu's older brother, Akira was nine years old and in 4th grade at Tokiwanishi School. His younger brother, Kozuo was three years old and attended kindergarten three days a week. Nobu, like Christopher was six years old. They sat next to each other in class. Christopher and Nobu become inseparable. They began visiting each other's homes, riding their bicycles together and going on long hikes together. I was thrilled to know that he'd found a friend.

One afternoon, Christopher came charging through the door, almost completely out of breath and asked,

"Mom, Watanabe-san has invited me to her house for dinner. Can I go?"

"Chris, I don't know about that."

"Please mom."

"Just a minute, let me call her."

"Moshi Moshi, Watanabe desu."

"Moshi Moshi, Watanabe-san. This is Chris-kun's *okasan*." (mother)

"How are you?"

"I'm fine thank you."

"How are you?"

"Fine, thank you."

"Watanabe-san, Christopher has told me that you and your family have invited him to join you for dinner. Is that true?"

"Yes, that's true. We'd love to have him join us."

"That's very nice of you. Thank you for having him."

"It's our pleasure. Christopher is such a nice boy and he and Nobu have become such good friends that we thought he might enjoy having dinner with our family."

"What time should he arrive?"

"We eat dinner at 6:30 PM."

"He'll be there."

"Thank you again, Watanabe-san. Goodbye."

"Goodbye."

I thought to myself, "This is very nice. Chris is having his first outing with a friend. He seems so happy to be joining his friend and his family. I knew this was the beginning of his assimilation into Japanese society and I couldn't have been more thrilled."

Soon thereafter, the Watanabe family began inviting him over on a regular basis. He attended play dates, birthday parties and even family outings. Whenever they invited him, he was always eager to go. He'd become so busy, I was actually seeing very little of him anymore. It was nice to see him forming friendships and enjoying himself outside of school. Spending time with Nobu and other children gave him the opportunity to begin sampling new foods. As a result of that, food was becoming less and less of an issue. He slowly began to acquire a taste for some of the local cuisine.

One morning, much to my surprise, he said,

"Mom, may I have miso soup and rice for breakfast?"

"Do you like miso soup?

"Yes, I had some at Nobu's house, and I like it."

"I think that's great. But, unfortunately, we don't have any miso."

"Do you think you could buy some?"

"I sure do. I'll buy some today after work and make it for you in the morning."

"That's great."

"Would you also like Japanese pickles and tea with your miso soup and rice?"

"Yes, I would. I like those too."

"Then we'll have miso soup, rice, pickles and tea for breakfast tomorrow."

"Thanks, mom."

"You're welcome."

He'd come a long way since the days of only bread and rice.

◆　　　◆　　　◆

He challenged me, yet again when he made a request for an *obento*. (An obento is a lacquered lunch box with small individualized compartments for packing a variety of foods.)

"Mom, I don't want to take a sandwich, cookies and chips for lunch anymore."

"You don't? Why not?"

"I'd like an obento, like my friends."

"Sweetie, I have to buy an *obento* box and then figure out what kinds of foods go inside. You'll need to give me some time on this one because I'll need to learn how to prepare the foods that go inside. That might take a few days, OK?

"That's OK."

◆　　　◆　　　◆

I called my good friend and neighbor, Hori-san.

"Moshi Moshi, Hori desu."

"Moshi Moshi, Hori-san, Stephanie desu."

"How are you?"

"I'm fine thank you, and you?"

"Fine, thank you."

"Hori-san, I need you help. Christopher has requested an *obento*.

"Honto?" (Really)

"Yes, really. I was wondering if you could help me learn to make one; that is to help me make some of the foods that would appropriate to put into an *obento*."

"I'd love to help you."

"If you tell me what kinds of foods go into the box, I can go to the grocer, and bring the ingredients with me to your home."

"That's good. I'll make a grocery list and have Mei bring it to your house."

"Is tomorrow good for you, Hori-san?"

"Yes, tomorrow's good."

"We'll see you tomorrow after dinner."

"I look forward to it."

"Thank you Hori-san."

"You're welcome."

"Goodbye."

"Goodbye."

Now that Christopher had acquired a taste for Japanese food and was beginning to make requests, I was committed to learning how to prepare everything he liked. Over time, Hori-san worked with me until I became a pretty good Japanese cook. Some of Christopher's favorite dishes were: *onigiri* (rice balls wrapped in seaweed) *edamame* (soybeans) *gomae* (steamed spinach with shredded carrots, soy sauce and sugar) *gyoza* (stuffed dumpling), *yakisoba* (a stir-fry made with noodles, vegetables and chicken or beef), *udon* (Japanese noodles), *miso soup*, curried rice and *sanma* (a flavorful oily fish with a consistency similar to salmon). I never tried to prepare sushi or tempura—those were delicacies I enjoyed at restaurants.

13

Back to *"buta."* I couldn't get that out of my mind. I was haunted by it night and day. At 5 feet 9 inches (5 feet 11 inches in heels), everyone in Japan told me how tall I was. I didn't mind being told that I was tall; I just didn't want to hear that I was fat. I decided, "It's time for a lifestyle change."

◆　　◆　　◆

Monday through Friday (and two Saturdays a month) Christopher left the apartment for school at 7:15 AM. Once he was out the door, I'd change into my jogging clothes and be out of the door myself and on the running track at about 7:30. I started slow, first with walking a mile every morning. Then, one mile became two, then three, then four. After several weeks of walking, I started running; first one mile, then two, then three. Within a couple of months, I was running four miles every morning except Sunday! Some mornings I'd run east in the direction of Tokiwanishi School and the rice fields; other mornings, I'd run west, in the direction of the farms and Go-zie-sho Mountains. When I ran east, I'd often come upon Chris and his friends as they walked to school. When they'd see me approaching they'd shout,

"Chris-kun's oka-san. Hello."

"Hello."

"Chris-kun's oka-san, Bye Bye."

"Bye Bye."

They were so cute. The only words in English they knew were "Hello and Bye Bye" and they were so proud to put them to good use.

Running became habit-forming. The more I ran; the more I wanted to run. I ran four miles in 45 minutes to an hour. By 8:15 or 8:30 I'd return home; shower, get dressed; eat breakfast and walk or ride my bike to work by 9:45.

◆   ◆   ◆

When I first arrived in Japan, I was challenged and (sometimes) intimated by grocery shopping. I couldn't read the labels or understand pricing. However, within a few months, grocery shopping became one of my favorite pastimes. I enjoyed discovering new foods and experimenting with new recipes. I began to change my entire attitude about food. I changed the way I shopped and I changed the way I ate.

A trip to the grocer became an adventure in itself. I soon learned that in Japan, there was no "Buy One—Get One Free," no "Jumbo," no "Family Size" no "25% More." I'd been accustomed to everything being sold in large or extra large packaging, but now I had to re-think sizing. I recalled the first day I walked through a grocery store and I said to myself, "Either I'm going to lose weight here or I'm going to die of starvation." (Well, I didn't die.)

I was forced to change my whole attitude about food. Food was expensive and everything in Japan seemed small—people, cars, houses and food. Even my refrigerator was small and my cabinet space was limited. Overnight, it seemed that I'd gone from "The Land of Giants" to "The Land of Lilliputians."

Limited storage space meant I could no longer afford to purchase large quantities of food at one time. In Japan, women shopped on a daily basis for fresh produce, fish, chicken and beef. Because I worked outside of the home, I didn't have the time to shop daily, but I did shop three or four times a week.

After I made the first two or three trips to the grocery store on foot and found myself struggling to carry home large packages, I decided to invest in a bicycle with a basket. That way, I could load my purchases into my basket and peddle to and from the store much faster and with greater ease. It was also a great form of exercise and aided in my weight loss.

14

With each passing day, life was becoming more peaceful; more sane. Christopher was happy at school; I was happy at work. However, as the school year progressed, the playground, once a lively little lot, was now completely void of children and had suddenly become a bastion of barrenness. Christopher came home one day and said,

"Mom, there's no one in the playground. Where are all the kids?"

"I'm not sure Christopher. Maybe everyone's inside studying." I asked Kanako.

"Kanako, we notice that there are no children in the playground after school anymore. Where do they all go?"

"During this time of year, the older children attend *juku* (Japanese cram school) or various after school activities. After school activities are a way of life for children in Japan. Everyone's busy doing something."

"Maybe I should enroll Christopher in a few of those activities."

"Maybe you should. I think it would be good for him. It's probably the only way he's going to see his friends after school."

"I think that's a good idea. It could also help to strengthen his language and could further help with his socialization."

"Can you provide me with the names of some of the after school tutors in our area?"

"I sure can. And the nice thing; they're all located right here in Yoko Dai, which means Christopher won't have to travel far for his lessons."

I enrolled him in Kumon two days a week. (Kumon is the method of learning math (and more recently reading) that originated in Japan in 1954 by Mr. Toru Kumon with a series of handwritten worksheets that he prepared for his son. It's tailored to meet each child's individual needs and abilities by giving them the freedom to progress at their own pace. The understanding was that children learned through practice and repetition.) He was enrolled in Japanese brush writing class two days a week, where he learned the ancient art of traditional Japanese scribing; piano lessons one day a week; and swimming class on Saturdays. The busier he was; the happier he seemed.

15

Music…the universal language; my vocabulary of choice; my form of communication; my passion. I grew up in an environment that was rich in music—all forms of music; classical, jazz, gospel, blues, rhythm and blues and country and western. My parents loved it all and I heard it all. I have fond memories of lying in front of the stereo in our living room and listening for hours to everything from Bach and Beethoven to Lerner and Lowe and from Rachmaninoff to the Rolling Stones. My grandmother played the harmonica; my father, the piano; and my mother sang. Music was in my blood. And as a child, I fell in love with the songs of Johnny Mathis, Sarah Vaughn, Ella Fitzgerald and Peggy Lee.

◆　　◆　　◆

One afternoon following class, Kanako approached me and said,

"Stephanie, Sam and I would like you and Christopher to be our honored guests at our annual celebration. Every year we host a party for family and friends and we'd love for you and Christopher to join us this year."

"Thank you for the invitation. We'd love to come. What do you need me to bring?"

"Nothing. You and Christopher are the "guests of honor," just bring yourselves."

"What time should we arrive?"

"The party usually starts around 7:00 PM. You can come anytime you like."

"We'll be there."

"So, we'll see you on Saturday around 7:00?"

"You sure will. I'm looking forward to it."

◆　　◆　　◆

Christopher and I arrived at the Winston home at about 7:30 PM on the day of the party. As we approached the house, we could hear the sounds of laughter and of live piano music emanating from inside. I thought to myself, "This sounds like a great party." We walked up the stairs and into the lobby where we removed our shoes, and went inside. We were immediately greeted by Kanako and Yumi.

"Welcome."

"Thank you."

"Please come and meet everyone."

Kanako introduced us to all her friends and neighbors. Everyone was so welcoming. And of course, everyone wanted to practice their English with me. It seemed I could never get away from teaching. Once a sensei; always a sensei.

Sam and all his friends were singing and playing their instruments. I made myself a drink and sat down in the living to enjoy the sweet sounds of music.

After a while, the pianist walked up to me, extended her hand and introduced herself.

"Hello, my name is Yuki. I hear that you're the new teacher from America who's here to work at Kanako's school."

"That's right. I'm Stephanie."

"It's nice to meet you."

"It's nice to meet you too. Yuki, you play beautifully."

"Thank you."

"How long have you played?"

"I started taking lessons when I was a child, but I don't think I'm very good."

In Japanese culture, individuals are extremely modest and slow to accept compliments. They tend to be self-effacing and view bragging and vanity as signs of self-centeredness.

"On the contrary, I think you play wonderfully."

"Well thank you Stephanie."

"Stephanie, may I ask you a question?"

"Yes, what is it?"

"I enjoy playing American jazz very much. By chance do you know *Misty*?"

"Do you mean—*Play Misty for Me?*"

"Yes, that's it."

"It happens to be one of my favorite songs."

"Can you sing it?"

"I can try."

We sat down at the piano. She took out her Great American Songbook, turned to *Misty* and started to play; I started to sing.

"Look at me, I'm as helpless as a kitten up a tree,
Never knowing my right foot from my left,
My hat from my glove, I'm too misty,

And too much in love."

When the other musicians heard us, one by one, they slowly began to chime in; first the bassist, then drummer and then the trumpeter. A hush fell over the room. All eyes and ears were upon us. Excitement was in the air. At the conclusion of our impromptu performance, everyone broke out in thunderous applause. Someone shouted: "Moto, Moto!" ("More, More!") I sang *Tea for Two*. Everybody loved it!

Yuki said, "Come Stephanie, let me introduce you to my friends.

"Stephanie-san, please meet Shin-san. He plays drums."

"I'm honored to meet you Stephanie-san. Welcome to Japan."

"Thank you Shin-san. It's so nice to meet you."

"This is Kenji-san and Yoko-san. Kenji plays guitar and bass and his wife Yoko plays trumpet."

"It's so nice to meet both of you."

"It's nice to meet you too."

"You all play so beautifully; I'm impressed."

"Well we think you sing beautifully. How long have you taken singing lessons?"

"I've never taken a lesson."

"You mean you've never had professional training?"

"No, never. I grew up in a music-rich home, so I've been exposed to music all my life. I just opened my mouth one day and started to sing. I guess it just comes naturally."

"That's incredible."

"Thank you for the compliment."

"Do you play an instrument?"

"I do. When I was college, I taught myself to play the guitar, so I could accompany myself when I sang."

"That's great. Did you ever want to sing professionally?"

"No. I never aspired to be a singer. I've sung at weddings, at church or at parties, but nothing professional. I enjoy it, so I just do it for fun."

Yoko said, "Stephanie, we all love American jazz music—we have a real passion for it. Many of our musician friends usually get together to rehearse every Tuesday night. We do it just for fun and to keep our skills up. Would you care to join us sometime?"

"I'd love to. But I don't know how I'd get to rehearsals. I don't own a car here."

"That's not a problem, my husband Kenji and I will gladly you pick you and Christopher up. Just give me your telephone number and tell me where you live. We'll pick you up at 6:45, rehearsal starts at 7:00."

"It sounds like a lot of fun. I look forward to seeing you on Tuesday night and I look forward to meeting more of your friends."

"We look forward to having you join us. I'm sure you'll have a great time."

◆   ◆   ◆

"Music is a more potent instrument than any other for education."

—Plato

When I went to Japan, I took my guitar along and I was glad I did. Music became my alternative means of communication while working with the children at the Montessori school. Music was proving to be one of my most powerful and effective teaching tools. When my students couldn't understand my words; they could always understand my songs. When they couldn't *speak* to me; they could always *sing* with me. Through my music I could engage them in a way that everyone could participate with each other and in a way that they could participate with me. It was magical. And although my youngest students didn't understand the words, they learned to sing American children's songs in perfect English, songs like *Eency Weency Spider, Old McDonald Had A Farm* and *She'll Be Coming Round the Mountain*, just to name a few. Through music, my students could move, and dance and express themselves. Through music I could deliver messages and I could entertain. Through music, I could speak; I could communicate.

◆   ◆   ◆

I started looking forward to Tuesday nights. For the first time in months, I'd found an interest in something outside of my work and outside of volunteering at Christopher's school.

On the Monday following the Winston's party, Yoko and Kenji telephoned me to get directions to our apartment. Yoko asked,

"Stephanie-san, what kind of music do you enjoy singing?"

"I like most everything, but I think my voice is best suited to singing ballads and old jazz tunes."

"That's very good. That's the music we enjoy playing most. We have a pretty large repertoire of music, so we just wanted to know what to bring with us tomorrow.

Like clockwork, they arrived at our apartment at 6:45 PM on Tuesday evening. Yoko rang the bell, I opened the door and she removed her shoes and stepped inside.

"Welcome to our home."

"Thank you."

I invited her in and offered her a seat.

"Yoko, I'll be ready in just one second. Just let me put Christopher's snack in a bag."

"You're OK. The studio is only about five minutes from here."

"Don't worry. I won't keep you waiting. Can I get you something to drink?"

"No thank you, I'm fine."

Yoko asked, "Stephanie, how do you like living in Japan?"

"I'm starting to like it a lot. And I love the people."

"Well, I have to say, that you've decorated your apartment beautifully. This is very nice; and very large for two people."

"You think this is large?"

"Oh it is. Normally, a family of three or four would occupy a space this size."

"That's interesting. Kanako said the same thing. So, I guess I shouldn't say anymore that Christopher and I live in a small apartment."

"No you shouldn't. This is quite nice."

"Thank you. Are you ready to go?"

"I am."

"Then let's go."

◆   ◆   ◆

Yoko was right. We drove south, all of five minutes and arrived at The Sapporo Music Studio right at 7:00. As Kenji pulled into the driveway, I was amazed at the size and the beauty of the building.

I said, "This is beautiful. Is it a new building?"

Kanako said, "It is. Construction was just completed on it about a month ago."

"May I have a tour?"

"I'm sure the owners would love to show you around. They're very proud of it."

We walked up the long stairway and rang the doorbell. We were greeted by a very nice couple—Ken and Saki Osagi. The Osagi's were the leading music promoters in the area. They had built the studio so that local musicians would have a place to practice and they supported themselves by renting out the space by booking concerts.

As the Osagi's opened the door to greet us, Yoko and Kenji made introductions and asked if I could take a tour of the premises. They were proud to show me around. The Sapporo Studio measured 4,000 square feet and sat on a main street, right in the heart of Yokkaichi's commercial district. The main area had three walls that were lined with full-length mirrors and the fourth was a wall of windows that looked out onto the main street. The floors were made a bamboo and the beautiful drop ceiling had four large ceiling fans. The studio was equipped with the latest state-of-the-art sound system and the acoustics were incredible.

After the tour, I was introduced to some of the other musicians and then we set up for rehearsal and practiced for an hour. I couldn't remember when I'd had so much fun and once again, found myself communicating through music!

On the drive back to our apartment, Yoko asked, "Stephanie, would you like to join us next Tuesday night?"

"Yoko, I'd love to."

"Then we'll see you next week."

"I'll be ready."

◆   ◆   ◆

Yoko and Kenji Fukushima and I started spending a lot of time together outside of rehearsals. They became two of my best friends. Some weeks following rehearsal, we'd go out for dinner together, and on weekends, Yoko and I often went shopping together. She also offered to drive Christopher and me to visit neighboring cities like Nara, Tsu City, Kuwana, Nagoya and Osaka for shopping and sightseeing. But the activity that we most enjoyed was shopping for food and cooking together. She taught me how to prepare some of her favorite Japanese dishes; I taught her some of my American favorites. Thanks to Yoko, I'm still pretty good at preparing Japanese foods.

During one of our cooking sessions, Yoko turned to me and said,

"Stephanie, would you be interested in performing a concert?"

"Really? Where?"

"At a local coffee house?"

"Tell me more."

"Kenji is good friends with the owner of C-Jay Coffee House. He told him about you and the owner asked Kenji if we'd like to perform there."

"That's exciting and it sounds like a lot of fun. I'd love to perform."

"Then I'll talk to Kenji and have him make arrangements and we'll get back to you."

"Yoko, that sounds great. I look forward to hearing from you."

◆   ◆   ◆

We prepared some of my personal favorites—*L-O-V-E, When I Fall in Love, Route 66, All of Me, Tea for Two, Jersey Bounce, Who's Got the Last Laugh and Besame Mucho.* We increased our rehearsal time to two days a week and continued practicing for another few weeks. We wanted to be sure we were in top form. Then Kenji made arrangements to book us at C-Jay Coffee House in Yokkaichi. We performed on a Saturday afternoon before an enthusiastic, sold-out crowd with standing room only. I was having the time of my life!

Word quickly spread throughout Yokkaichi and neighboring cities that "an American jazz singer" was in town! Invitations for us to perform started pouring in from everywhere. We had dates to perform at other coffeehouses, at restaurants, at jazz clubs and at private parties.

I'd traveled to Japan to teach English as a Foreign Language, and there I was gaining a reputation as jazz singer—how funny was that?

◆   ◆   ◆

Christopher and I had finally become part of a larger community. We'd been accepted and embraced by everyone inside and outside of Yoko Dai. We were no longer "the new kids on the block." The novelty of our presence in the community had long worn off. We were no longer viewed as tourists; no longer viewed as visitors. We were just like everyone else—we were residents; we were neighbors; we were home!

16

Life was good; we were happy; we were comfortable; we were content. Although Christopher and I were making friends and adjusting to our new life, I realized that I could no longer procrastinate when it came to my Japanese lessons. I was proud of the fact that I'd acquired quite an extensive vocabulary, but a vocabulary wasn't enough. I needed to be able to string those words together into a sentence and have the ability to converse. I called Kanako.

"Kanako, do you know of anyone who could tutor me in Japanese?"

"As a matter of fact I do. I have a friend, Ota-san who speaks English quite well. She and her husband own the large restaurant across the street from the Yu Store near downtown Yokkaichi. I know that she'd like to improve her English so maybe the two of you can work something out. Maybe you can practice your Japanese and she can practice her English."

"That sounds like a good idea. May I give her a call?"

"Please do. I'm sure she'd love to hear from you."

"Thank you Kanako."

"You're welcome."

The Yu Store was a beautiful, large, upscale department store near downtown Yokkaichi. Christopher and I had visited there on numerous occasions, so when Kanako told me that the Ota family lived directly across the street from the Yu Store in the large restaurant called Mo-Mo Taro, I knew exactly where that was.

I telephoned Ota-san the following day.

"Moshi Moshi, Ota desu."

"Moshi Moshi, Ota-san. This is Stephanie Allen. I work at Kanako Winston's Montessori school. She said it was OK for me to call you regarding Japanese lessons."

"Yes, Stephanie, Kanako told me you'd be calling. Would you like to make arrangements to meet?'

"I'd love to. What day is good for you?"

"What about Saturday afternoon at 4:00 PM?"

"Four o'clock is a good time."

"That's good. I thought we could practice speaking Japanese for 30 minutes and then practice speaking English for 30 minutes."

"Yes, I think that would be great."

"Would you like to come to my house?"

"I could do that."

"Do you know where I live?"

"I do. Kanako told me that you live in the large building with the Mo-Mo Taro structure on top, directly across the street from the Yu Store. Is that the place?"

"That's the place. The restaurant's on the lower level; we live on the upper level."

"Then, I'll see you on Saturday. Oh, by the way Ota-san, is it OK if I bring my son Christopher along?"

"Sure you can. He can play with my boys while we study."

"Thank you, Ota-san. I look forward to meeting you and to working with you."

"I look forward to working with you also. I'll see you on Saturday at 4:00 PM."

"Goodbye."

"Goodbye."

◆   ◆   ◆

Christopher and I arrived at Ota-san's home on Saturday afternoon at 3:55. We rang the doorbell; she opened the door and welcomed us to her home.

"Konnichiwa." ("Hello.")

"Konnichiwa." ("Hello.")

"Ogenki desuka?" ("How are you?")

"Genki desu." ("I'm fine.")

"I'm sorry, Ota-san. That's about the extent of my Japanese."

"Actually, that was very good."

"Thank you. I want to get better."

"That's what you're here for. Let's start with Japanese, and then we'll switch to English."

"That sounds good."

Ota-san was a great teacher. Our Japanese session was intensive and fast-paced. She didn't allow me to write things down or to use my dictionary. She said that the best way to learn was by speaking repetitively. She was hard-driving and she set the bar really high for me, but it forced me to learn quickly.

During the Japanese sessions, I told Ota-san that I wanted to learn how to converse or ask questions, especially when I found myself in certain situations while running errands—to the bank, at the grocer, at the train station. Ota-san said, "I'll teach you what you need to know, plus a lot more. And you'll be surprised at how much you'll learn."

"That's great. Let's get started."

The first lesson was one in how to introduce myself and my son, and then she taught me how to answer the telephone at work.

"Watashi wa Allen Stephanie desu." ("I am Stephanie Allen.")

"Konoko wa watashino musuko desu." ("This boy is my son.")

"Na ma e wa Christopher desu." ("His name is Christopher.")

"Amerika jin desu." ("I'm American.")

"Chicago kara kimashita." ("I come from Chicago.")

And then, for answering the telephone at the Montessori school—

Me: *"Moshi Moshi, Montessori Sho Gakko."* ("Hello, this is the Montessori School.")

Caller: *"Moshi Moshi. Winston-san, kudasai?"* ("Hello, may I speak with Mrs. Winston?")

Me: *"Do chira sama desuka kudasai?"* ("Who's calling please?")

Caller: *"Shimizu desu."* ("This is Mrs. Shimizu.")

Me: *"Chotto matte, kudasai."* ("Just a moment please.")

Prior to this, I'd always panic whenever the telephone rang at work; especially when Kanako wasn't available. But now, I no longer had a fear of answering when Kanako was out of the room. I wasn't as proficient as Christopher, but I was doing quite well.

And then, Christopher became my source of inspiration. Whenever he had the opportunity to hear me speak Japanese, he always said,

"Gambatte kudasai, okasan." ("You're doing good, Mom, keep your chin up!")

17

Through language, we acquire the ability to understand and the ability to *be* understood. Without the ability to communicate, we feel lost, we feel isolated; we feel disconnected. We learn to speak by *hearing* speech spoken repetitively, day in and day out. Through our exposure to speech, we learn the repetitive patterns, rhythms and nuances of our families, our friends and our community.

◆   ◆   ◆

One evening while we were visiting Kanako, Christopher (like he'd done so many times before) went in to Yumi's room to play with she and her friends. The girls always felt free to talk among themselves (even in Christopher's presence) because they knew he couldn't understand their conversation. But this time, it was different. This time, when they giggled, he giggled. When they spoke again, he giggled again. The more they talked, the more he giggled. Finally, Yumi called out to her mom, "Momma, I think Christopher can understand what we're saying."

Kanako (not at all being surprised) turned to Christopher and asked him a question in Japanese.

"Sumimasen, anata no o na ma e wa nan desuka?" ("Excuse me, what is your name?")

"Boku no wa Christopher desu." ("My name is Christopher").

"Nihongo o hanoshi masuka?" ("Do you speak Japanese?")

"Watashi wa Nihongo o sukoshi hanoshi masu." ("I speak a little Japanese.")

I couldn't believe my ears; the girls couldn't either. Everyone except for Kanako was surprised. She knew that in time, he would learn to speak Japanese. She was right. And according to Kanako, not only did he speak Japanese, but he spoke it with a *Yokkaichi bin* (a regional dialect). I was so proud of him.

It seemed that all those months of observing and listening to his teachers and to his friends had finally paid off. And from that moment on he just seemed to change right before our eyes! With each passing day, he became happier and more confident. And when he was happy; I was happy!

◆   ◆   ◆

We faced our moment of truth on a beautiful, sunny Saturday morning. Christopher and I made plans to take the train to downtown Nagoya for the day. We rode our bicycles to the train station; locked them up and purchased our tickets. The train was running late. Normally, we'd wait five or six minutes; however, this time, our wait was about 20 minutes long. When the train finally arrived, it was much more crowded than usual. We couldn't find two seats together, so we sat directly across from each. At the next stop, a *(toshiyori)* an elderly lady boarded the train. The gentleman seated next to Christopher stood up and offered her his seat. She sat down, turned to Christopher and said,

Mori-san: "Konnichiwa." ("Hello.")

Christopher: "Konnichiwa." ("Hello.")

Mori-san: "Ogenki desuka?" ("How are you?")

Christopher: "Genki desu!" ("I'm fine, thank you.")

Mori-san: "Anata no na ma e wa nan desuka?" ("What is your name?")

Christopher: "Boku no na ma e wa Christopher desu." ("My name is Christopher.")

Christopher: "Anata no na ma e wa nan desuka? ("What is your name?")

Mori-san: "Watashi wa Mori desu." ("My name is Mrs. Mori.")

Mori-san: "Gakusei desuka?" ("Are you a student?")

Christopher: "Hai." ("Yes.")

Mori-san: "Nan sai desuka?" ("What is your age?")

Christopher: "Na na sai desu." ("I'm seven.")

Mori-san: "Nan nensei desuka?" ("What year are you in school?")

Christopher: "Ni nensei desu." ("I'm in second grade.")

Mori-san: "Gakko no na ma e wa nan desuka?" ("What is the name of your school?")

Christopher: "Tokiwanishi sho gakko." ("Tokiwanishi School.")

Mori-san: "Sensei no na ma e wa?" ("What is your teacher's name?")

Christopher: "Nori Sensei desu." ("Nori-san.")

Mori-san: "Anata wa otoko no go-kyodai ga o-ari desuka?" ("Have you any brothers?")

Christopher: "Iie, otoko no kyodai wa imasen." ("No, I have no brothers.")

Mori-san: "Anata wa onna no go-kyodai ga o-ari desuka?" ("Have you any sisters?")

Christopher: "Iie, onna no kyodai wa imasen." ("No, I have no sisters.")

Mori-san: "Genkide ne." ("Take care of yourself.")
Christopher: "Genkide ne." ("Take care of yourself.")
Mori-san: "Gambatte kudasai." ("Keep your chin up. Do good.")
Christopher: "Domo arigato goziemasu." ("Thank you very much.")
Mori-san: "Sayonara Chris-kun." ("Good-bye, Christopher.")
Christopher: "Sayonara Mori-san." ("Good-bye, Mrs. Mori.")

I sat there with my mouth open in amazement, listening to their conversation and beaming with pride.

I knew he was beginning to speak, but I had no idea just how fluent he'd become. He'd conversed with Mori-san with such poise, such ease and such confidence that it sounded as if he'd been speaking Japanese all his life. I'd never had the opportunity to hear him speak because he only spoke to me in English. At that moment I thought back to the day I'd suggested pulling him out of Tokiwanishi and enrolling him in a school where English was spoken. However, after witnessing the interaction with Mori-san, I was glad that Kanako had convinced me to leave him where he was.

Christopher had become fluent in Japanese out of need. It had been out of a need to connect with his peers; out of a need to communicate; out of a need to form friendships. And not only was he learning to speak Japanese; he was also learning to read and write in Japanese!

◆   ◆   ◆

We'd arrived in Japan at a critical time in Christopher's development. In 1992, he was six years old and had just completed kindergarten. At the time we'd arrived, he was on the verge of reading and writing, but he'd not yet mastered either. When he learned to read and write—it was in Japanese!

In Japan, there are four methods of writing. They are:

- *Hiragana* which is the first and the simplest form that is taught to young children. Children's books are typically written in Hiragana only.

- *Katakana* is mainly used for writing non-Japanese words or names that can't be written in Kanji.

- *Kanji* which is the most advanced system of Japanese writing that utilizes characters borrowed or adapted from Chinese writing.

- *Romaji* which is written using English lettering for the convenience of foreign-ers. English speakers can read and write Japanese without learning Japanese writing. (The Japanese words in this book are written in Romaji.)

Christopher learned to read and write using hiragana and katakana characters, and he also learned a few characters in kanji.

◆　　　◆　　　◆

His fluency in Japanese was not only beneficial to him; I benefited also. The more proficient he became; the more I depended on him to translate for me. And although I'd learned a great deal from Ota-san, I didn't speak with the same level of confidence that he did. He had total comprehension and could move in and out of English and Japanese with total ease. Now I needed his help. I needed to order a taxi to take me downtown to meet a friend for lunch.

"Christopher, I need to take a taxi downtown. Can you order it for me?"

"Sure mom. What time do you need it to pick you up?"

"I need it to be here at 1:15 PM."

I gave him the telephone number to the taxi company. He dialed the number; told the operator he was ordering a taxi for his mother; gave them our address and placed the order for 1:15.

The true test would be whether or not the taxi would show up. It did.

I looked out at 1:15, and the taxi was waiting downstairs!

Christopher and I went downstairs together; he went to Kanako's house; I climbed into the taxi.

After lunch, I went to Kanako's to pick Christopher up. Kanako asked me,

"So, Stephanie, what do you think about Christopher's speaking ability?"

"I have to say that I'm absolutely thrilled. But I'm also shocked and amazed. And needless to say, I'm very proud of him."

"Are you happy you left him at Tokiwanishi School?"

"You don't *know* how happy I am. You told me he'd be fine and he is. It was indeed a struggle in the beginning and I have to admit that I couldn't see the light at the end of tunnel, but this has truly worked out. I'm so glad I listened to your advice."

"I knew he'd do it. We're very proud of him too."

"And just think, had I taken him out of Tokiwanishi, he probably wouldn't have established such strong friendships in the neighborhood either. I have to say again; I'm so happy I listened to your advice."

"Now that we're on the subject of friends in the neighborhood, I have a funny story to tell you."

"What is it?"

"When I told the families in Yoko Dai that an American child would be moving into the area, they were all very happy."

"Why so?"

"They saw it as an opportunity for their children to learn to speak English."

"Did that happen?"

"No, not really. And on the contrary, Christopher became fluent in Japanese!"

"That *is* funny. But I hope they're not disappointed."

"No, they're not at all. Everyone's proud of Christopher and they all see you and Christopher as a real asset to our community.

"That's very nice. Thank you."

18

It had been almost a year since my young student had referred to me as *buta*. So, needless to say, I found myself beaming with pride when a friend asked,

"Stephanie, have you lost weight?"

"As a matter of fact, I have. Does it show?"

"Does it ever. How much have you lost?"

"I've lost 50 pounds!"

"You've lost that much?"

"Yes I've lost that much."

"Was it difficult?"

"No, not at all. On the contrary, it was quite easy."

"How'd you do it?"

"I did it by eating right; eating light and jogging every day."

"Well, you look absolutely wonderful. Keep up the good work."

"I will. And thank you for the compliment."

The Japanese have one of the healthiest diets in the world, and I'd adhered to that same diet. I ate rice, skinless chicken, fish with bones, soy products, fresh fruits and vegetables, green tea and dried seaweed. I consumed very little red meat, partly because it was higher in fat, and partly because it was very expensive. I jogged and rode my bicycle everyday and as a result, the pounds just melted away!

◆　　　◆　　　◆

I now needed a new wardrobe and a new hairstyle to complement my new body; my old image just didn't suit me anymore. My first thought was, "But where in Japan am I going to find clothes long enough to fit my 5 foot 9 inch (175-cm) frame? And worse yet, where am I going to find a hair salon with a stylist who'll be able to (or willing to) style my hair?"

By nature, I'm an extremely optimistic person. However, when it came to finding clothes to fit me in Japan, my optimism was beginning to fail me. But, I ventured out, just that same. I said, "Maybe I'll get lucky." My first stop was Hitachi, an upscale department store in downtown Yokkaichi. I rode the escalator to the second floor and as soon as I stepped off and turned to my right, I couldn't believe my eyes, there was a huge sign with blue lettering that read: *Tall Girl's Boutique!* I couldn't believe it—a tall girl's boutique in Japan! I thought, "This is great!" I was so excited, I could hardly contain myself. I took two pairs of slacks, two shirts, two dresses and two blazers into the fitting room. I tried on a pair of slacks (a size 10) and they fit me "like a glove." This was a surprise to me because the last time I'd tried clothes on, I was a size 16! I was so happy, I tried on everything, but I only purchased the two pairs of slacks and the two shirts. I walked out of Hitachi Department Store feeling like "a million bucks." I felt like I was "walking on a cloud." My confidence had been restored. Next stop, shoe salon. I walked into Miyazaki Shoe Store. The sales clerk greeted me. He took one look at me and then, one look at my feet.

"Iie, Iie, ashi okii!" ("No, no, big feet!")

I couldn't believe he was telling me that my feet were big! I mean, I knew they weren't exactly small, but I didn't think they were that big either. But then, I had to remember, I *was* in Japan. Maybe my feet (like my body when I first arrived) were considered big by Japanese standards. I was so embarrassed that I just turned around and walked out. "Oh well," I thought, "I'll just try another shoe salon. I did. No luck there either. "I know; I'll just go back to Hitachi. If they could fit me in clothes, surely they'll have shoes in my size." No such luck. I thought, "Surely, I can't be the only woman in Yokkaichi with big feet. It was very frustrating.

I went home and called my friend Osaka-san to ask for advice.

"Osaka-san, I have a question for you."

"What is it?"

"What's the average shoe size for women in Japan?"

"Japanese women have really small feet. The average size for women ranges from 36-39."

"Let's see, I think that converts to sizes 5-8 (U.S.)"

"What size do you wear in America?"

"I wear a size 10."

"Here in Japan, a size 10 converts to a 41. A size 41 is a man's size."

"I can't believe that."

"It's true. So what are you going to do?"

"I guess I'll have to call my mother and ask her to ship me some nice shoes."

"I'm sorry Stephanie-san."

"No need to apologize, Osaka-san; it's not your fault. Having my mom to ship me shoes won't be a problem at all. I can just describe to her what I like and she can pick them up. I'm sure I'll have them in a few days."

I could change my body size, but I couldn't change my shoe size. I'd seen so many pretty shoes in the shop windows, so it was disappointing to not be able to find anything that would fit me. I just called my mom and asked if she could buy me a pair of running shoes, a pair of pumps and a pair of strappy sandals.

◆   ◆   ◆

I hadn't done very much to my hair since I'd arrived in Japan almost a year ago, and I'd definitely not seen the inside of a styling salon. The changes in climate and water had finally taken their toll and my hair was beginning to show signs of neglect. Its structure, texture and condition had also changed. My natural curls, which were once full of luster, shine and elasticity, were now dull, dry and lifeless. And for the past year, my hair care regimen had been simply to shampoo, condition and let it air dry. But now I needed more; I needed help. And unbeknownst to me, help was on the way.

Masuda-san and his wife were friends of Kanako and they owned the hair salon on Adachi Avenue. They'd noticed Christopher and I as we'd walked past or ridden our bikes past their shop. They immediately assumed that I was the new teacher from America who was in the country to teach at the Montessori Language School. Mr. Masuda called Kanako.

"Kanako-san, this is Masuda desu. Do you have time to talk?"

"Yes Masuda-san. How can I help you?"

"I have seen an American lady and a young boy walk by our salon on numerous occasions. By chance, is she the new teacher at your school?"

"She is. That's Stephanie and her son Christopher."

"Well, I would love to style Stephanie-san's hair. Do you think she'd allow me to do that?"

"I don't know. But if you'd like, I can ask her."

"If she's interested, would you please have her call me to make an appointment for a consultation?"

"I'll do that. I'll give her your number and have her give you a call tomorrow."

"Thank you."

"You're welcome."

"Goodbye."

"Goodbye."

Masuda-san had received his training in Europe, and although he'd worked with all types of hair (except African-American hair), he specialized in Japanese hair. When he caught sight of me (or when he caught sight of my hair) he'd called Kanako.

When I arrived at work the following morning, Kanako told me that she'd spoken with Masuda-san from the salon on Adachi Avenue.

"Masuda-san called me and asked me to ask you if he could style your hair."

"Do you think he can style *my* hair?"

"I don't know, but he's willing to try. Here's his number. Why don't you give him a call and make an appointment for a consultation."

"I can speak a little Japanese now, but does he speak English."

"He does. He speaks fairly well."

"That's good. I'll give him a call. I have to say, I appreciate his willingness to work on my hair. That's admirable."

"He's very good. I think you'll be pleased."

I telephoned Masuda-san the following day.

"Hello Masuda-san?"

"Yes."

"This is Stephanie Allen from the Montessori School. Kanako Winston gave me your telephone number. She said you that you're interested in styling my hair."

"Stephanie-san, I'd love to work with you. Would you like to come in for a consultation?"

"I'd like that very much. Is tomorrow at 4:00 PM good for you?"

"Tomorrow at 4:00 it is. I'll see you then."

"Goodbye."

"Goodbye."

Masuda-san's shop was small (only four chairs), but it was very nice; very modern. He examined my hair and told me that he could definitely work with me. I was pleased to know that. Although my hair is naturally curly, he told me that its texture was more like Japanese hair than not. He said he would use a process called "Japanese Straightening" or "Thermal Reconditioning." I admired his enthusiasm and his willingness to try something new. I agreed to allow him to style my hair. I made an appointment for the following day.

I arrived at the salon at 4:00, after my last class. I changed into a spa robe and sat down in the first chair. Masuda-san excused himself and went into rear to mix together the ingredients for the relaxer that he'd apply to my hair. Several minutes later he returned with the cream relaxer and several flat plastic boards. Starting at the nape of my neck, he divided my hair into small sections and using a flat brush, spread the cream relaxer onto the hair while stretching it over flat plastic boards. He used the longer boards at the back and on the sides and the shorter boards on the top. When he completed that process, I sat for 20 minutes, and then he put me under the dryer for 30 minutes. When I came from under the dryer, he removed the flat boards, shampooed me, applied a deep conditioner and then put me back under the dryer for another 30 minutes. Afterwards, he took me back to the shampoo bowl, rinsed out the conditioner, clipped my ends, blew it dry and styled it. The entire process took about three hours. But the results were worth it! My hair was in the best condition ever.

"Masuda-san, this is absolutely beautiful. Thank you."

"You're welcome. It was easy."

"How long should this last between treatments?"

"This process should last you four or five months. You need only come in from time to time for a basic styling—shampoo and conditioning."

As I walked home, I felt proud; I felt pretty. It was the first time in a long time that I'd felt the breeze flowing through my hair.

The following day, everyone said,

"Wow, Allen sensei, your hair looks beautiful."

"Thank you. Thank you very much."

19

The spring of 1993 was quickly drawing to a close and Kanako would be starting her search for a new teacher for the 1993-1994 school year. So, I was rather surprised when she approached me and asked,

"Stephanie, do you have any plans for next year?"

"No I don't. Not yet anyway."

"Well, if you don't have any plans, would you be interested in returning to Japan next year?"

"I'm surprised you're asking me. I thought you were only interesting in having teachers for one year."

"Normally I would be, but it seems like things are working so well for you and Christopher that I thought you might be interested in staying on. If you'd like to, we'd love to have you."

"You know Kanako, I hadn't thought much about it, but seeing as Christopher has adjusted so well and has made so many friends, I think another year would be good."

"Thank you for the offer."

"Thank you for accepting."

"It's nice to know that I'll have a job next year."

"Do you and Christopher plan to return to Chicago over the summer?"

"We do. It's been a year since we've seen family and friends. I'm looking forward to going back."

◆　　　◆　　　◆

The end of our first year in Japan meant that Christopher and I had reached another major milestone.

At the beginning of our journey, I didn't how things would turn out. I didn't even know if we'd make it through to the end of the year. But what a difference a year had made. We'd been through a lot; especially Christopher, but somehow, we'd come out unscathed. I was proud of us and all that we'd accomplished in one short year. In that year we'd experienced a kaleidoscope of emotions; everything from anger to frustration and from embarrassment to fear, and somehow, we'd conquered them all!

We'd struggled in our new environment and we'd questioned everybody and every-thing. But in the end, it had all been worth it.

In the beginning of the first year, I'd had a frightened, unhappy and confused little boy who wanted nothing more than to return to his home in the U.S. But by the end of the year, that same little boy had learned a new language, assimilated into a new culture, had adjusted to a new environment, and was now a happy, healthy, well-adjusted little boy. We'd both had rich, rewarding, life-altering experiences.

Through careful observation, by listening and by asking questions, he and I had learned a great deal about the people and the culture of Japan and it had served us well.

And it was with great anticipation that we were looking forward to our second year.

It was now time to return to Chicago and share our experiences with our family and friends.

◆   ◆   ◆

I called my friend Haruko.

"Hello. This is Haruko."

"Hello Haruko. This is Stephanie."

"Stephanie, how are you my friend?"

"I'm fine. How are you?"

"I'm doing great."

"That's good to hear. Haruko, I was calling to ask a favor of you."

"What is it?"

"I was wondering if you could drive Christopher and me to the airport in July. We'll be returning to Chicago for the summer."

"I can do that. Just let me know the date and time."

"I'll get back to you when I have the details."

"Stephanie, you'll be coming back right?"

"Oh, yes. We're just going for the summer. We'll return in August."

"That's good. We're not ready to lose you and Christopher just yet."

"You don't have to worry."

"Like I said, please call me when you have the details about your trip."

"I'll do that. And thank you Haruko."

"You're welcome."

"Let's talk soon."

"Let's do that."

"Goodbye."

"Goodbye."

This time when we flew, I was much more prepared. I knew how to dress comfortably and I knew to bring along *onigiri* (rice balls) *and edamame* (soy beans) just in case Christopher wouldn't eat the food on the plane. We were much more comfortable and much more relaxed on our return flight. He never complained of tummy aches or headaches. And he actually slept most of the way (which meant I too got to sleep.) We arrived at O'Hare International Airport feeling much more relaxed that we had when we arrived at Nagoya International Airport the year before.

◆   ◆   ◆

Everyone back in Chicago was happy to know that we'd be coming home; it had been a year, and it did feel good to be going home to spend time with family and friends. I was really looking forward to it.

My mother met us at the airport. She was so glad to see us. Her face lit up when she saw us coming through the gate. Christopher ran into her so hard, he almost knocked her off her feet. They hugged for what seemed like forever. She then turned to me. I gave her a big hug and a kiss. The first thing she said was,

"Steph, you're so skinny." (I wasn't skinny at all; it's just that when she'd last seen me, I was six sizes larger.)

"I've lost weight, but I don't think I'm skinny at all."

"How'd you do it?"

"It was quite easy. It was the first time I've lost weight naturally and without dieting. I simply consumed less food; I ate healthy food and I exercised."

"Well, you look fabulous."

"Thank you mother. You look fabulous too."

"Thank you, dear."

As we went to claim our bags, I took a look around the airport. It had only been a year, but everything seemed so different; the people seemed different; the environment seemed noisier; the pace was faster; and people weren't as pleasant as the people in Japan had been. In just one short year, I'd become accustomed to a much slower, quieter pace and accustomed to people who seemed much nicer and were much more gracious; much more accommodating. I was home again, but in many ways, I was experiencing "reversed culture shock."

But in spite of everything, being back in Chicago felt good. I realized that there was a lot about the city that I'd missed—the Magnificent Mile; the lake; the music scene; and that fabulous skyline! We claimed our luggage and loaded everything into the car. I asked my mom,

"Do you mind if I drive?"

"Please, be my guest."

It felt good to be behind the wheel again; it had been a year since I'd driven a car. My mom and I talked the entire way to her home. We had a lot of catching up to do. My mom said, "Everyone's waiting to see you and Christopher."

"We're waiting to see them too."

"They'll be surprised at your weight loss."

"I hope they like it; I know I do."

We stayed at my mother's house, but we had plans every day to see someone; family members, friends or former co-workers. Being home again, we found ourselves being just as busy trying to fit everyone in as when we'd left a year before.

It seemed like all we did was answer questions. Everyone wanted to know how we liked it; how I liked my job; and how Christopher was doing school. I had nothing but good news.

But the real talk of the town was my incredible weight loss. Most people thought I looked really good; really healthy, but others thought that I'd lost too much. Those were the opinions I ignored.

After about three weeks, I found myself feeling anxious and wanting to get back to Japan. I was actually feeling homesick for Yokkaichi! We'd only lived there for a year, but in that time, we'd adjusted to well and we felt so happy, that it now felt more like home than Chicago! After three weeks, when I told Christopher that we'd be returning to Yokkaichi in a week, he just said, "OK mom." For him, it was like going home also because it was where his school was, where his friends were and where his bike was. He couldn't wait to get back either. It had been a great summer, but soon it would be time to say goodbye.

I finally broke the news to my mom that we'd be returning to Japan.

"Mother, just in case you were wondering, we're planning to return to Japan for another year. What do you think about that?"

"Somehow, I'm not surprised. I knew you were planning to stay for a year, but somehow, it seemed like whenever I spoke with you by telephone, you always seemed so happy and you always said that Christopher was doing so well. So no, I'm not surprised at all. As long as you're happy and Christopher's happy, that's all that matters."

"You don't know how happy it makes me to hear that. Having your blessing makes everything seem alright. We are having a wonderful time and I'm actually looking forward to going back."

"Well you just go back and enjoy yourself. This is a great opportunity, and you're deserving of it."

"Thank you so much."

The following week, we found ourselves once again, saying goodbye for another year, loading luggage into a car; and taking off for the airport. Traveling the world with my young son was becoming a way of life. But it was a way of life that I'd come to enjoy.

◆   ◆   ◆

For some reason, our return flight was only half full. The flight attendant approached us and said,

"Miss, we don't have a full flight today. If you'd like, you and your son can move to the center section which has bigger rows. That way, you'll be free to spread out and relax."

"Thank you. That's very kind of you to offer. I appreciate it."

Christopher and I took our things and moved to the center section. (which had five seats across.) We removed our shoes and spread out. It really was much more comfortable. Having the opportunity to lift the arm rests and elevate my legs made all the difference in the world. This time, when we arrived in Nagoya, I was much more rested and Christopher was much less irritable than we'd been a year before. In just one short year, he and I had become experienced travelers.

◆   ◆   ◆

When we reached Nagoya International Airport the following day, the customs agent asked,

"What is your business here in Japan?"

"We live here."

"Welcome home."

"Thank you."

He stamped our passports; we claimed our luggage and walked out of the exit. This time there was no one waiting to pick us up. This time, we were home. So, we hailed a taxi and asked the cabby to drive us to our apartment at 4-1 Greenhill Yoko Dai in Yokkaichi.

◆   ◆   ◆

We were back in Yokkaichi and making plans to begin our second year. In the second year, we picked up where we'd left off. In the second year, life was much more sane; much more predictable; much more peaceful.

I went back to teaching at the Montessori school and Christopher went back to second grade at Tokiwanishi School. All of our friends and neighbors were happy that we'd returned, just as we'd said we would.

20

Food, like language, was no longer an issue for us. We no longer feared food, and we no longer struggled with the language. Over the past year, Christopher and I had become extremely close with our musician friends, Yoko and Kenji. Food, like music, had become a central part of our relationship. We dined together, either at one another's home or at a different restaurant two or three nights a week. Not only did Yoko and Kenji teach us about food, they taught us about the culture of food in Japan. Whenever we dined at their home, they'd always introduce us to new foods. Their dinners consisted of full course meals starting with *miso* soup and rice, *niza-kana* (fish that had been simmered in a stock flavored with soy sauce), sugar and *mirin* (sweet sake), *nuka-zuke* (vegetables such as cucumber and eggplant that have been pickled in a salty rice-bran paste), and *croquettes* (balls of mashed boiled potato mixed with minced meat and onion, dipped in a thick batter then deep-fried). *Biru* (beer) was served at every dinner. It's customary as a gesture of politeness or a show of respect to pour a drink for the person seated next to you, who in turn pours your drink. After the drinks have been poured, everyone says, *"com-pai"* ("cheers"), and then everyone takes their first sip together.

Before eating a meal we said, *"Itadaki-masu"* ("I will receive and thank you to the cook"), and after eating a meal we said, *"Gochiso-sama"* ("Thank you for the delicious meal.") By observing others, Christopher and I learned the proper way to serve ourselves and the proper way to use chopsticks. We also learned that making a slurping sound while eating noodles or drinking soup was appropriate.

Rice was usually eaten plain or with a few drops of *sho-yu* (soy sauce) or a seasoning made from nori (seaweed). The Japanese never use gravy or butter on rice.

With each passing day we learned new lessons in food consumption. Learning *how* to eat was as important as learning *what* to eat. Observing others and asking questions helped us to learn appropriate behavior while dining in friends' homes or in restaurants. In Japan, proper etiquette can often appear to be very different from what's considered proper etiquette in the U.S. And in many cases, the opposite applied. For example, drinking directly from your soup bowl without using a spoon was not considered inappropriate. We also learned that *o-hashi* (chopsticks) are held in the right hand and the bowl in the left. Chopsticks on large plates are used for bringing food to your plate. However, if serving chopsticks are not available, then it's appropriate to use the large end of your chopsticks (the end that does not go into your mouth) to bring food to your plate. We learned that it's inappropriate to use chopsticks like mallets or drumsticks by tapping on the table. And one should never hold the bowl and chopsticks with the same hand. We were told that we should never spear or stab our food with our chopsticks, and never pull a bowl or plate toward us with our chopsticks.

◆   ◆   ◆

I learned that understanding and respecting the culture of food and by knowing the appropriate behavior when dining was as important (if not more so) than speaking the language.

21

The Japanese believe that the most important goal for all institutions is the establishment harmony (*wa*). This harmony is of key importance within the family, the school and the community. Expectations and requirements for children and adults are very much the same. By Japanese standards a *good* child is one who is compliant, mild-mannered, open-minded and cooperative.

The Japanese value effort over achievement and harmony over conflict. They also focus on a student's attitude and behavior. In Japan, society views itself from the point of view of a *good* child and a *good* citizen.

In our community of Yoko Dai, most households were comprised of a mother, father, and one, two, or three children. A small number of households were comprised of a husband and wife but no children, and others were comprised of extended families, that included maternal or paternal grandparents. It is understood that when the oldest son in a family marries, he and his wife will live with *his* parents so that he and his wife will become his parents' caretakers as they grow into old age. Young women usually live at home until they marry.

In Japanese culture, there is little emphasis on the individual. Everyone sees himself or herself as part of their *family*. And when individuals go to school and later to work, they view themselves as part of a *group*. When individuals introduce themselves or when they introduce others, they do so by saying the family name first. For example: "Watashi wa Hattori, Keiko desu." ("My name is Hattori, Keiko.") As a show of respect, Christopher and I began introducing ourselves in the same way. For example "Watashi wa Allen, Stephanie desu or Boku no wa Allen-Bradley, Christopher desu."

From a very early age, children are taught that they are one with the family and therefore must behave accordingly. Any negative or inappropriate behavior could bring shame on the entire family. Children are taught to behave appropriately at all times so as to not embarrass the family.

A large part of our indoctrination into Japanese culture was in becoming a part of the community, while learning about and participating in the different elaborate ceremonies and festivals that took place throughout the year. I felt it was important for us to participate in as many of these celebrations as we could because they would help to define the people and the culture of Japan.

Here are some of the important holidays and ceremonies that were celebrated in Japan:

- *Coming-of-Age Ceremony (15 January)*

The Coming-of-Age Ceremony is a national holiday that honors young adults who are twenty years old—the year before they enter into official adulthood. Special ceremonies are held throughout the country for young adults and their parents.

- *Setsubun (2 or 3 February)*

Setsubun is the eve of the first day of spring. People toss roasted soybeans outside of their houses while chanting "*oni-wa-soto!*" ("Out with the devil!") Beans are scattered in the house while chanting "*fuku-wa-uchi!*" ("In with good luck!") Then, for a year of good luck, some of the bean are eaten—the same number as your age.

- *Hina Matsuri (Girls' Day) (3 March)*

Hina are dolls that represent the emperor, empress, and members of the ancient Japanese court. Girls are given the dolls at birth and they put them on display in their homes every year.

- *Children's Day (5 May)*

The 5th of May was celebrated as Boys' Day in the past, but it is now a national holiday to celebrate all children. A family with a boy displays a miniature set of medieval Japanese armor inside the home and a set of flying carp streamers outside.

Other festivals are: *Tanabata* (7 July), Summer Festivals (July and August), The Bon Festival (13–16 August), Athletic Meets (September or October), Harvest Moon Viewing (September's Full Moon), *Shichi-Go-San* Festival (15 November), Christmas Eve, Christmas Day, and Year's End.

Friends or neighbors invited Christopher and me to all the festivals and celebrations. We ate traditional foods, sang traditional songs, and sometimes wore traditional clothing. It was a fabulous opportunity for us to learn about all aspects of Japanese culture and the Japanese way of life.

◆   ◆   ◆

Our second Christmas in Japan was quickly approaching. And it was turning out to be as much fun and as festive as our first Christmas had been. Although 99% of the country was Buddhist, Christmas was still celebrated (although commercially) in a big way. On Christmas Eve, parents put presents near children's heads while they slept. Christmas is not a national holiday, but office parties were common during the holidays. Many of our friends put up a Christmas tree, but decorations were confined to indoors. Christmas was celebrated, not as a religious holiday, but as an opportunity to enjoy oneself and to provide gifts for children. Each year we were there, I wanted to make Christmas as magical and as memorable for Christopher as I possibly could. I bought a tiny little tree, decorated it and asked him for his "Wish List."

Our first year in Japan, Christopher asked,

"Mom, does Santa Claus come to Japan?"

"Of course, Santa Claus comes to Japan. Santa Claus goes everywhere in the world. Don't worry. Santa knows you're here. He won't forget you."

Following the success of the first year, I had no problem convincing him that Santa would arrive for the second year. And once again, all his wishes were granted.

◆   ◆   ◆

The biggest and most festive of all the celebrations in Japan are New Year's Eve (*Omisoka*) and New Years Day (*Ochogatsu*).

By 31 December, people thoroughly clean their homes and put up decorations to symbolize happiness. Pine trees (*kadomatsu*) were set up at the gates of homes, and ferns, mandarin oranges, a kelp and lobsters were hung over the front entrance. At midnight, temples all over Japan ring 108 strokes on their bells. On New Year's morning everyone celebrated by partaking of a spiced wine (*otoso*) and rice cakes boiled with vegetables (*ozon*) and other foods. People throughout Japan are filled with a sense of renewal and exchange the familiar greeting: "Akemashite Omedetou Gozie-masu" (Happy New Year!) During the first three days of the New Year (*sanga-nichi*) and the first seven days (*matsu-no-uchi*) people make New Year calls to acquaintances and relatives or they send New Year cards. Government offices, firms and other businesses resume operation on 4 January.

Children looked forward to receiving New Year's gifts (monetary) from parents, grandparents and other relatives.

After all the shopping had been done, everyone went about the business of cleaning the home and then preparing all the traditional Japanese foods. Families begin gathering at one another's homes to celebrate the New Year with food, drink, song, dance, and games like "Go," "Shogi," and "Sugoroku."

"Go" is the most often played on a square board with 9, 13 or 19 horizontal and vertical lines intersecting to form a square grid. The object of the game is to control territory on the board. Occasionally you may capture your opponent's pieces, but it is usually less profitable than capturing territory.

"Shogi" is Japanese Chess. To "checkmate" the opponent's king, a "check" occurs when the king is under direct attack. A checkmate is a situation where the opponent's king is under attack and completely trapped.

"Sugoroku" is Japanese Backgammon. The object of the game is to clear one's pieces from the board first. Players take turns rolling a pair of dice and can either move a single disk the number of spaces of the total dice roll or two disks each the number of one of the dice. The first player to clear all of his pieces from the board is the winner.

Friends and neighbors always made Christopher and I feel like a part of their families by inviting us to join them on New Year's Eve and New Year's Day. Food for the New Year is distinctly traditional, usually served in *jubako* (tiers of square, lacquered wooden boxes). One fish that is sure to be served is *tai* (red snapper), red being the color of good fortune and *medetai* (a joyous occasion). Food for many meals is prepared by 31 December so that the women too could be free from kitchen duty during this most festive time of the year.

PART III

Going Home Again (Kikoku)

o o o o o o o o o o o o o o o o o o o o o o o o o o o o o o o o o o o o

"Hold fast to your dreams, for if dreams die, life is broken like a winged bird that cannot fly."

—Langston Hughes
www.quoteland.com

22

The time to say goodbye was upon us. From the moment we'd arrived in Japan, I knew this day would eventually come. And so, here it was. What I didn't know was that saying goodbye would be so hard. Preparing to say goodbye was causing me much anguish, sorrow and grief.

All those months ago, I'd made the journey for myself because at the time, it had seemed like the right thing to do for me. However, I'd remained on this journey for my son, because once again, it had seemed like the right thing to do for him. In 1992, opportunity had knocked and I'd answered the call. I'd followed my heart and fulfilled a dream.

I'd decided that a second year would be more beneficial for Christopher than it would be for me, and so I'd returned. He'd adapted and had excelled academically, socially and emotionally; and he was at peace.

I'd traveled to Japan with the intention of staying for one year. But one year had turned into two, and at one point, I'd even thought about making it three; but I in my heart, I knew it was time to go.

And as I look back on that time, all those years ago, I'm reminded of the happiness and the joy that we experienced, and the wonderful people that we met along the way. I'm reminded of how much we learned and how much we were transformed—physically, mentally and emotionally.

Once I'd made the decision to leave, I had to come to terms with my decision. And then there was the added stress of having to share my decision with Kanako, and then with Christopher.

For several months I'd toyed with the idea of returning to the U.S. But I knew I could no longer put it off. I finally mustered up the courage to tell my friend.

"Kanako, do you have time to talk?"

"Sure. Let's go upstairs to the kitchen. What is it?"

"Unfortunately, the time has come for us to return to Chicago."

"I'm sad to hear that, but I knew this day would come."

"I'm really torn. We're so happy here and we love it so much."

"I know you do, and we love having you. But I understand."

"Kanako, I want you to understand that a large part of the reason why we're going back is because Christopher is not reading or writing in English and I'm concerned about that."

"And rightfully so. I can understand your concern."

"At eight years old, his "window of opportunity" for learning to read and write is getting smaller and smaller. The older he gets, the harder it'll be for him to learn."

"Believe me Stephanie, you don't need to apologize. As a mom and as a teacher, I can definitely understand what you're saying."

"I feel bad that I'm leaving you "high and dry.""

"Well, you're not. Don't worry about me and don't worry about the students. We'll miss you, but we understand it's what you have to do. Everything will be fine."

"It makes me feel good to hear that. You've been so good to us. I'd hate to think that I'm letting you down."

"I'd never think that. You need to go so you can focus on Christopher now."

"Thank you. And thank you for understanding."

Now that I'd shared the news with Kanako, it was time to tell Christopher. I kept trying to think of when would be the best time to tell him. But there really was no *best* time. I just had to tell him. One evening during dinner I just said it.

"Christopher, I have something to tell you."

"What is it, Mom?"

"We'll be going home soon—this time to stay. This time we won't be coming back to Japan.

"What do you mean, Mom? We're already at home."

"No, I mean we'll be going back to the U.S.; back to Chicago."

He started to cry.

"Mom, why do we have to go? I'm happy here. All my friends are here; my teachers are here; my school is here. I like Japan."

"Christopher, we didn't come here to stay forever. Now we have to go back."

"Why can't we just stay?"

I felt so bad; so guilty. I'd be uprooting him yet again and starting over—yet again. There was nothing I could do. I knew that children tend to be more resilient than adults, and they have the ability to adapt to new environments, but I still felt guilty about disrupting his world—a world he'd grown to love. He'd come so far in the past two years; he was so happy; he was so content. Hearing him; made me cry. We were so sad. "Christopher, let's try and get through this so you can finish your dinner."

"I'm not hungry mom."

"Maybe you can finish later when you feel better."

The next day he went to school and told his teachers and his friends that he'd be returning to America. He'd been with Nori Sensei for the past two years for 1st grade (*ichi-nensei*) and 2nd grade (*ni-nensei*.) Recently he'd been promoted to the 3rd grade (*san-nin-sei*) and had a new teacher, Higashi Sensei. Several weeks earlier when I'd met Higashi sensei, he'd said to me,

"Allen-san, I'm thrilled to know that Chris-kun will be in my class. I have heard some great things about him and I'm looking forward to working with him."

"Thank you Higashi-san. I'm happy to meet you and I'm happy to know that you're looking forward to teaching Christopher. He has indeed come a very long way in the past two years."

So needless to say, Higashi Sensei was shocked to hear that we were planning to leave Japan. When he got the news, he called me on the telephone.

"Moshi Moshi, Allen desu."

"Moshi Moshi, Higashi desu."

"Hello Higashi-san. Is Christopher OK?"

"Christopher's fine; but I'm not. I just got the news that you'll be leaving Japan. Is that true?"

"Unfortunately it is."

"Why are you leaving?"

"It's time. As hard as it's going to be to leave, we really have to get back now."

"We were all shocked to hear that you're leaving. Christopher has been here so long and has progressed so much. I guess we just thought he'd be here forever."

"Overall Higashi-san, how's he doing in third grade?"

"He's doing great. A few of his friends from ichi-nensei and ni-nensei have moved into the same class with him, but most of the students are from neighboring classrooms. But he's still doing extremely well and has made some new friends."

"How's he doing academically?"

"He's doing extremely well. I'm so impressed with his progress. And when I talk to him, I notice that his speech patterns, his mannerisms, his attitude, and his behavior are very much like those of a Japanese child. And he speaks Japanese extremely well. I still can't believe he's leaving. We're going to miss him so much."

"This is not easy for any of us, but the time has come to return to the U.S."

◆   ◆   ◆

The following day I started informing friends and neighbors that we'd be leaving within a month. It made me sad because all of our friends were so sad. In 1992, I had no idea that our arrival in Yokkaichi would have such an impact on the community; and now two years later; we were having a similar impact, but this time, it was a negative impact. I'm convinced that everyone just assumed that we'd stay on forever.

We were leaving; not because we *wanted* to, but because we *had* to. Although Christopher was doing extremely well in school, I really couldn't afford to keep him on any longer. For the past two years, I'd tried to no avail to encourage him to read; to teach him to read, but he'd expressed little to no interest in reading or writing in English. In his mind, he didn't have a need to read in English because everything he read, wrote and spoke was in Japanese. I tried to convince him that reading and writing in English was also important, but he'd have no part of it. I'd brought along all of his books, and had even purchased more while we were there. He enjoyed cuddling with me every night while I read to him, but when I tried to encourage him to read along, he had no interest. But now that he was eight years old, it was time to get back and start working on his English proficiency. I was impressed with his fluency in Japanese (and it was important that he maintain that ability) but it was equally as important for him to move as freely through reading and writing in English. I felt that the longer we stayed in Japan, the harder it would be for him to readjust to the American school system.

◆   ◆   ◆

I was becoming all too familiar with subletting apartments, donating furniture, packing bags and relocating. When I'd done it two years before, I had feelings of anxiety and fear, but the excitement and anticipation far outweighed any feelings of apprehension. However, this time, there was a level of sadness in the air; this time it wasn't by choice; this time, it was because we *had* to leave.

As I cleared out the apartment, I was amazed at how much "stuff" we'd acquired in two years. Several days prior to leaving, I had our larger items and some of my more delicate pieces shipped to Chicago by UPS. We'd arrived in Japan with four pieces of luggage; we were returning with six.

◆   ◆   ◆

The day of our department finally arrived. We had an 8:00 AM flight. We were up bright and early at 5:00 AM. I walked out on our patio and looked to east in the direction of the rice fields and Tokiwanishi School and gazed at what would probably be my last Yokkaichi sunrise. Kanako was scheduled to drive us to the airport at 6:00 AM. Christopher and I got dressed and had a light breakfast.

When we finished our breakfast, Christopher occupied himself by playing with his Legos while I applied my makeup. Our doorbell rang. I wondered to myself,

"Who could that be? We're not expecting anyone (not yet anyway.") I called out,

"Just a minute please."

"Mom, who's that?"

"I don't know. Kanako's not expected for another half hour or so."

I went to the door and opened it.

I was shocked. It seemed like all of my students, their parents and everyone in the community had come by to bid us farewell.

"Allen sensei, we wanted to say goodbye to you and Christopher."

I was so moved by this display of love, respect and admiration. And in a move that is uncharacteristically Japanese, everyone started hugging us and crying, which just made me cry even more. When I started to cry; Christopher started to cry. My makeup started to smear, and I never got a chance to complete the application. I was a mess, my eyes became red and puffy and my head started to ache.

"Allen sensei, please promise us that you and Chris-kun will come back to Japan."

"We will. We promise. We'll come back."

I didn't know how to tell them that I had to go so that I wouldn't miss my plane. But then, just in time, Kanako intervened. She had to push her way through the crowd and she said to everyone,

"I'm sorry to have to break this up everyone, but Stephanie and Christopher have an 8:00 flight. We don't want them to miss it."

"Thank you for coming everyone. Christopher and I want to thank you for everything. We'll never forget you, and we *will* come back."

"Goodbye Allen Sensei."

"Goodbye everyone."

At that point, it was just easier to remove my make-up as opposed to trying to apply it to my tear-stained face. I washed my face; gave Kanako the key to our apartment; grabbed our luggage; went downstairs; loaded everything into the car; and drove north out of Yoko Dai to Nagoya International Airport.

23

We spoke different languages. We had different cultures. Yet we shared the same goals, the same aspirations and the same dreams. Much to my surprise, I learned that we had much more in common with the people of Japan than I'd originally thought. Over time, I came to realize that people really are more alike than they are different.

Our cultural exchange taught me that no matter where we are in the world; no matter what language we speak or culture we claim; we share the same basic needs and have the same basic desires—a need for family; a need for friendship; a need for belonging.

When Christopher and I traveled to Japan in the summer of 1992, we had no idea what we were in for; no idea what to expect. In the beginning, we were strangers in a strange land, totally dependent on the kindness of others for support; for validation; for confirmation. In the beginning, we felt inadequate, incompetent and insecure. We knew nothing and we feared everything. But over time, all of our fears, all of our inadequacies, and all of our insecurities were replaced with confidence, self-assurance and poise. But the best and most exciting part of our journey was the one we took with the people of Japan who loved us and embraced us and made us feel like we were home. It was those people who'd started out as strangers and who became our friends for life.

We came away from Japan with a new attitude; a new way of thinking and with new feelings about ourselves and about the world. The experience of having lived in Japan helped Christopher and I become more compassionate, more understanding, more resilient and more accepting of others.

We came away with a new appreciation for a different country; a different culture, and a different people. We were extremely fortunate and felt honored to have had the opportunity to share two years of our lives with such a gracious, loving and generous people who (without hesitation) had opened their hearts; their minds and their homes to us and had welcomed us with open arms.

In 1992, I'd traveled to Japan to *teach;* what I *learned* was priceless. I took with me an open mind; a positive attitude and unlimited optimism. I returned with a heightened sense of spirituality, patience and peace. Our experience had truly been a *Magnificent Exchange* of languages, cultures, customs and beliefs.

◆　　　◆　　　◆

I was proud of the fact that I'd faced my fears—the fear of the unknown, the fear of flying overseas and the fear of living abroad (and I'd conquered them all.) And now that I'd faced my fears; I felt I could face any challenge, any time, any place or anywhere.

Since our return, the two questions that have been asked of me, time and time again are,

"Do you regret having lived in Japan?"

"I have no regrets. It was the most incredible experience of my entire life. It was absolutely wonderful."

"If you had the opportunity to do it all over again, would you?"

"If I had the opportunity to do it all over again, I'd do it in a heartbeat!"

Epilogue

In two relatively short years, Christopher and I had adopted a new country; a new culture and a new lifestyle.

Leaving Chicago for Japan had been one of the biggest and most difficult challenges I'd ever faced. Leaving Japan to return to Chicago had been no less challenging; no less difficult.

I would have thought that coming home would have been a celebration of sorts; something that we both would have been ready for and something we both would have looked forward to. But instead, coming home had posed a whole new set of problems—seen and unseen. Christopher had to prepare himself for yet another change; another transition. He would now be forced to *learn* some new things; *unlearn* some old things and *relearn* others. And once again, he was at a disadvantage.

We arrived in Chicago in late spring, and although we were quickly approaching the end of the school year, I wanted to enroll him in 3rd grade, even if just for a few weeks.

◆　　　◆　　　◆

I called the principal at Sterling Elementary School and introduced myself.

"Mr. Blake, my name is Stephanie Allen. My son Christopher and I have just moved back from Japan. He's eight years old and I'd like to make an appointment to meet you and your staff and make arrangements to get him enrolled."

"Is tomorrow morning good for you and Christopher?"

"Tomorrow would be good. What time should we arrive?

"Is 9:00 AM good for you?"

"It is."

"Then we'll see you then. Just check in at the main office and ask for me."

"Thank you Mr. Blake. I look forward to meeting you."

"I look forward to meeting you and Christopher."

"Goodbye."

"Goodbye."

◆   ◆   ◆

Christopher and I arrived at Sterling Elementary at 9:00 AM and reported to the main office. We checked in with the receptionist.

"Good Morning."

"Good Morning."

"My name is Stephanie Allen; this is my son Christopher. We have a 9:00 appointment with Mr. Blake."

"Please have a seat. I'll let Mr. Blake know you're here."

Mr. Blake came out right away. As he approached, Christopher and I stood up and shook his hand. Mr. Blake was extraordinarily tall and slim (about 6 feet 4 inches.) He had a pleasant face, thinning mixed gray hair and soft brown eyes. He wore a light green suit with a darker green tie and a soft yellow shirt. He walked out of his office and extended his right hand.

"Welcome to Sterling Elementary. I'm the principal, Mr. Blake."

"It's nice to meet you Mr. Blake."

"Let's step in to my office."

When we walked in there were two other women present. They stood as we entered the room.

"Good morning. I'm Mrs. Jacobson. I'm the Vice Principal."

"It's nice to meet you. I'm Stephanie Allen, and this is my son Christopher."

"Good morning Christopher."

"Good morning."

"And I'm Mrs. Benson. I'm one of the third grade teachers."

"It's nice to meet you to."

Mr. Blake told his assistant to please hold his calls for the next hour while he met with us, and he closed the door to his office.

"Ms. Allen tells me that she and Christopher have just returned from Japan where Christopher has been enrolled in a Japanese school for the past two years. She'd now like to enroll him in 3rd grade here. I chose you Mrs. Benson because I think you would be the perfect teacher to work with him."

Mrs. Benson was a very small, petite woman with short dark hair and dark eyes. Mr. Blake chose her because she was considered one of the school's finest teachers—she was celebrating 20 years as an elementary teacher. When I met her, I thought, "I'm confident that Christopher will be in good hands here."

I said, "I'd like for all of you to know that Christopher completed a portion of 1st grade, all of 2nd grade and a portion of 3rd grade while in Japan. When we arrived in Japan, he was on the verge of reading and writing in English. However, when he learned to read and write, it was in Japanese."

Mrs. Benson said, "That's very interesting. But if you're concerned about it, don't be. It won't be a problem at all. He's still at an impressionable age where he will learn quickly. Please know that we'll work with him. We'll get him enrolled and he can start tomorrow. You can talk to Mr. Blake to find out what documents he'll need for getting registered. And if you'll excuse me, I have to get back to my classroom, but I look forward to seeing you and Christopher tomorrow morning."

"Thank you Mrs. Benson. We look forward to working with you."

◆   ◆   ◆

Christopher was eager to get back in school; I was eager to have him there. It was important that he maintain some sense of order and routine.

Mrs. Benson was wonderful. With knowing that Christopher wasn't reading or writing yet, she provided him with as much extra help as she could.

What she noticed though was that he struggled with reading and writing, but he excelled in math. When I went to school one day to pick him up, she said,

"Ms. Allen, I administer an activity that I call "The Math Minute." I give the children worksheet with 50 addition, subtraction or multiplication tables and they try to solve as many problems as they can in a 60-second time period. Well, what I've noticed is that Christopher performs all three operations with amazing speed and accuracy. He's always the first one to finish. How do you explain his incredible ability?"

"He was enrolled in Kumon for two years."

"Well that explains it."

"I'm happy to know he's doing well in at least one subject."

"Oh, he's doing extremely well. And don't worry, he'll also be reading and writing in no time at all."

All of the children in Mrs. Benson 3rd grade class were reading and writing at or above grade level. When the children realized that Christopher was struggling to read and write, they began taunting him,

"Chris can't read; Chris can't write; Chris is dumb."

Mrs. Benson said, "Just a minute boys and girls. We don't call anyone dumb in this classroom. And you should know that Christopher can indeed read and write; it's just that he reads and writes in Japanese. And soon he'll be reading and writing in English as well."

Christopher was very upset by hearing his classmates refer to him as "dumb." Once again, he was overwhelmed and was left feeling devastated, humiliated and embarrassed.

I got a telephone call from Mrs. Benson.

"Ms. Allen, I've been thinking and I'd like to make a suggestion."

"What is it?"

"You might think it a little odd, but please, hear me out."

"I'm all ears. And at this point, I'm open to most anything."

"What would you think of enrolling Christopher in an English as a Second Language (ESL) Class? We offer them here at Sterling."

"Oh, Mrs. Benson, that does sound rather odd."

"Maybe it doesn't. Let's look at it this way, Christopher has been immersed in Japanese culture for the past two years—two very crucial years; two formative years. Most children learn to read and write between 1st, 2nd and 3rd grades. His thought patterns, speech and nuances are like those of a Japanese child. English is the first language he learned to *speak*, but it's the *second* language he'll learn to read and write. So, in many ways, English *is* like a second language to him."

"That's very interesting, and very true. You make a very good point. I'm willing to give it a try. It couldn't hurt."

We enrolled him in an ESL class three days a week.

◆   ◆   ◆

After a few weeks, I received another call from Mrs. Benson.

"Ms. Allen, this is Mrs. Benson."

"Hello Mrs. Benson."

"How's Christopher doing these days?"

"That's the reason for my call."

"Please tell me. Is it good?"

"Oh, it's great! Today in class, I asked for a volunteer to read the first paragraph in our Weekly Reader Magazine. And guess what?"

"What?"

"Christopher raised his hand to volunteer."

"Mrs. Benson, that's fabulous."

"I was so proud of him. He stood up and read the first paragraph like he'd been reading for years. I was so proud of him. And it great that his classmates had the opportunity to hear him read."

"You don't know how happy I am to hear this."

"Yes I do. And I'm happy too. But you know who's most proud?"

"Who's that?"

"Christopher. He was so proud of himself. And that's what matters most."

"You're absolute right Mrs. Benson. And thank you."

"It's my pleasure. And I have to say, it's moments like these that make teaching worth it."

◆   ◆   ◆

At eight years old, Christopher was fluent in two languages. And I felt it was important for him to maintain his fluency. He'd acquired a unique and wonderful skill set and I wanted to do everything within my power to provide the supports that would help maintain his skills. I was proud of his accomplishments and the ease with which he could transition in and out of English and Japanese.

I contacted the Japanese Consulate in Chicago to inquire about Japanese lessons for him. They referred me to a Saturday school at the Buddhist Temple for Japanese Language. I enrolled him there. The school offered classes every Saturday morning from 10:00 AM to 12 noon. The students were from metropolitan Chicago and its surrounding suburbs and they ranged in age from 6 to 16. They practiced conversational Japanese and they learned to read, write and compute in Japanese.

In conjunction with the Japanese Consulate, the Buddhist Temple also sponsored an annual speech competition. The children were required to write their own speeches, read them to a panel of distinguished judges and then they were expected to answer a series of questions that related to their speech. Christopher won first place for two consecutive years; and in the third year, he came in second.

◆   ◆   ◆

Once again, I contacted the Japanese Consulate, to inquire about student referrals.

"Moshi Moshi, Hello. Japanese Consulate."

"Moshi Moshi. My name is Stephanie Allen. I was calling for information."

"Yes, how can I help you?"

"I have just returned from Japan, where I taught English as a Foreign Language. I'm now back in Chicago, and I'm interested in offering private English lessons to Japanese nationals. Does the Consulate make referrals?"

"We do. But we need to know more about you. Do you think you can come in to the Consulate tomorrow?"

"I can. What time is good for you?"

"Ten o'clock is good. Do you know where we're located?"

"Yes I do."

"We'll need you to bring a copy of your resume, your social security card and license and the name of your employer in Japan. Can you provide those things?"

"I can."

"Then we'll see you tomorrow at 10:00 AM.

"I look forward to meeting you. And thank you very much."

"Goodbye."

"Goodbye."

The following day, I met with the Director. I completed an application and provided her with the required documents. After she processed my application and checked my references, I signed a contract and the Consulate referred me to several students in my community. I designed a curriculum and tailored it to meet the needs of each individual student. I charged an hourly rate and offered private English lessons four or five days a week

◆   ◆   ◆

Christopher and I returned to Japan in the summer of 1996 when he was 10 years old. I went over for a two-week visit and took him to participate in a four week home stay program. He spent the summer with his friend Nobu and the Watanabe family. He got re-acquainted with all his old friends and had the opportunity to re-enroll at Tokiwanishi school for 5th grade (*go-nensei.*)

His 5th grade sensei was Miyagi-san. She remembered him from before and said she was looking forward to having him in her class. I wondered how he'd perform and if he'd be able to pick up where he'd left off two years before. Kanako called the school and asked to speak with Miyagi sensei.

"Miyagi sensei, this is Kanako Winston."

"Hello Winston-san. How are you?"

"I'm doing well, thank you."

"How can I help you?"

"I'm just calling to get a progress report on Christopher."

"Well, Chris-kun is doing extremely well."

"Does he seem to understand the lesson and is he following directions?"

"Yes, he's doing just fine."

"Does he still read and write?"

"He does. He's reading and writing quite well. He's just picked up right where he left off two years ago. It's as if he's never skipped a beat. He's a real joy. We're all very happy to have him back at our school."

"That's good to know. I'll be sure to pass this information on to his mother. I'm sure she'll be pleased."

"Thank you for calling."

"Thank you."

"Goodbye."

"Goodbye."

After two weeks, I returned to Chicago. After four weeks, Christopher returned with our friend Osaka-san. She then spent two weeks at our home before returning to Japan.

◆   ◆   ◆

It's been years since Christopher and I left Yokkaichi Japan. But our special bond to the people and to the country has never been severed. And our friendships have endured forever.

◆   ◆   ◆

Christopher is now a 20 year old college sophomore. He's majoring in business with a minor in Japanese. He continues to speak Japanese and he still enjoys Japanese cuisine. He and I have plans to return to Yokkaichi for two weeks in the summer of 2006 and we're looking forward to once again connecting with all of our old friends.

Japanese Pronunciation Key

There are five vowels in Japanese:

a   i   u   e   o

Sounds like:
  "*a*"—as in: "*ma*"
  "*i*"—as in: "*he*"
  "*u*"—as in: "*moo*"
  "*e*"—as in: "*may*"
  "*o*"—as in: "*toe*"

Vowels combined with consonants are written as follows:

a	i	u	e	o			
ka	ki	ku	ke	ko	kya	kyu	kyo
sa	shi	su	se	so	sha	shu	sho
ta	chi	tsu	te	to	cha	chu	cho
na	ni	nu	ne	no	nya	nyu	nyo
ha	hi	fu	he	ho	hya	hyu	hyo
ma	mi	mu	me	mo	mya	myu	myo
ya		yu		yo			
ra	ri	ru	re	ro	rya	ryu	ryo
wa	(w)i		(w)e	(w)o			
ga	gi	gu	ge	go	gya	gyu	gyo
za	ji	zu	ze	zo	ja	ju	jo
da	ji	ji	de	do			

| ba | bi | bu | be | bo | bya | byu | byo |
| pa | pi | pu | pe | po | pya | pyu | pyo |

Japanese—English Glossary

A

Amerika—America
arigato—thank you
arigato gozaimasu—thank you very much
ashi—foot

B

Bon Festival—Celebration for the departed
biru—beer
boku wa—"I am" (used by young boys)
buta—pig

C

chan—term of endearment for children as in Miki-chan
chotto matte—just a moment please
compai—"cheers!"

D

dake—only
dochira sama—"who's calling?"
domo arigato—thank you very much
doko desuka—where

E

edamame—soybeans

F

fuku wa uchi—"in with good luck"

G

gakko—school
gakusei—student
gai-jin—foreigner
gambatte—keep your chin up; do good.
ginko—bank
Go—Japanese board game
gochi-so-sama—thank you for the delicious meal
go-kyodai—brethren; sisters; brothers
gomae—steamed spinach with carrots, sugar and soy sauce
gomen nasai—I'm sorry
Goziesho—Mountains in Yokkaichi

H

hai—yes
Hina Matsuri—Doll's Festival
hiragana—simplest form of Japanese writing

I

ichi-nen-sei—third grade
ikura desuka?—how much?
itadaki-masu—I will receive this food and thank you to the cook.

J

jubako—square, lacquered wooden boxes

K

kanji—Chinese characters
katakana—A form of Japanese writing
kojo-sensei—school principal
kon-ban-wa—good evening
konoko—boy
kotatsu—low table used for dining
kudasai—please
Kumon—instructional method for teaching math and reading

M

manga—Japanese animation
matsu-no-uchi—the first seven days of the New Year
medetai—a joyous occasion
mirin—sweet sake
miso—soy paste
mizu kudasai—water please
MONBUSHO—National Government Education Board in Japan
moshi, moshi—hello (when answering the telephone)
musuko—son

N

Nagoya—city in Honshu
na ma e—name
Nanzan University—major university in Nagoya
nansai—how old?
Nara—ancient capital of Japan from A.D. 710 to 784
ni nen sei—second grade
niza-kana—fish simmered in a stock flavored with soy sauce, sugar and mirin
nori—dried seaweed
nuka-zuke—vegetables picked in a salty rice-bran paste

O

o-daijini—take care of yourself
obento—boxed lunch
Ochogatsu—New Years Day
ofuro—bath; bathtub
ogenki desuka—how are you?
ohashi—chopsticks
okasan—mother
okii—big; large
Omisoka—New Year's Eve
onigiri—rice balls; sometimes wrapped in dried seaweed
oni-wa-soto!—Out with the devil
onna—female; woman
Osaka—one of the commercial and industrial centers of Japan
otoko—male; man

R

ran-do-seru—backpack; knapsack
roku-nen-sei—sixth grade
romaji—Romanized Japanese writing

S

sanga-nichi—the first three days of the New Year
sanma—an oily fish; ideal for grilling
sayonara—goodbye
san nen sei—third grade
sensei—teacher
Setsubun—February 3rd. Eve of the first day of spring
shichi-go-san—(7-5-3)—November 15. Celebration of 3, 5 and 7 year-olds
sho-yu—soy sauce
sugoroku—Japanese backgammon
sukoshi—a little; a little bit
sumimasen—excuse me
Suzuka City—a city in Japan

T

tai—sea bream
Tana bata—July 7—Star Festival
tatami—mat; matting
tomodachi—friend
Tokiwanishi—local public school in Yoko Dai
Tokyo—capital city of Japan
toshiyori—elder; aged person
Tsu City—a city in Japan

U

udon-dake—plain udon; udon only

W

watashi wa—I am

Y

yaki-soba—stir fry made with noodles, vegetables and chicken or beef
Yokkaichi—a city in Japan; the largest city in Mie Prefecture
Yokkaichi-bin—regional accent
Yoko Dai—a community in Yokkaichi

Basic Japanese Vocabulary

Numbers

1	—	*ichi*
2	—	*ni*
3	—	*san*
4	—	*shi*
5	—	*go*
6	—	*roku*
7	—	*shichi*
8	—	*hachi*
9	—	*kyu*
10	—	*ju*
11	—	*ju-ichi*
12	—	*ju-ni*
13	—	*ju-san*
14	—	*ju-shi*
15	—	*ju-go*
16	—	*ju-roku*
17	—	*ju-shichi*
18	—	*ju-hachi*
19	—	*ju-kyu*
20	—	*ni-ju*

Months of the Year

January	—	*Ichi-gatsu*
February	—	*Ni-gatsu*
March	—	*San-gatsu*
April	—	*Shi-gatsu*
May	—	*Go-gatsu*
June	—	*Roku-gatsu*
July	—	*Shichi-gatsu*
August	—	*Hachi-gatsu*
September	—	*Ku-gatsu*
October	—	*Ju-gatsu*
November	—	*Juichi-gatsu*
December	—	*Juni-gatsu*

Days of the Week

Monday	—	*Getsu-yobi*
Tuesday	—	*Ka-yobi*
Wednesday	—	*Sui-yobi*
Thursday	—	*Moku-yobi*
Friday	—	*Kin-yobi*
Saturday	—	*Doyo-bi*
Sunday	—	*Nichi-yobi*

Colors		
red	—	*aka*
blue	—	*ao*
yellow	—	*ki*
green	—	*midori*
orange	—	*dai-dai*
black	—	*kuro*
white	—	*shiro*
pink	—	*mo-mo*
purple	—	*murasaki*
gray	—	*hai*
brown	—	*cha*

Time		
1:00	—	*ichi ji*
2:00	—	*ni ji*
3:00	—	*san ji*
4:00	—	*yo ji*
5:00	—	*go ji*
6:00	—	*roku ji*
7:00	—	*shichi ji*
8:00	—	*hachi ji*
9:00	—	*ku ji*
10:00	—	*ju ji*
11:00	—	*juichi ji*
12:00	—	*juni ji*

Directions		
North	—	*Kita*
South	—	*Minami*
East	—	*Higashi*
West	—	*Nishi*

Money		
Y 1	—	*ichi yen*
Y 5	—	*go yen*
Y 10	—	*ju yen*
Y 50	—	*go ju yen*
Y 100	—	*hyaku yen*
Y 500	—	*go hyaku yen*
Y 1,000	—	*sen yen*
Y 5,000	—	*go sen yen*
Y 10,000	—	*ichi man yen*
Y 50,000	—	*go man yen*

Mealtime		
breakfast	—	*asa gohan*
lunch	—	*hiru gohan*
dinner	—	*ban gohan*

The four seasons		
winter	—	*fuyu*
spring	—	*haru*
summer	—	*natsu*
fall	—	*aki*

Basic Japanese Greetings and Phrases

Good Morning.	*Ohayo Gozaimasu.*
Good Afternoon (Hello)	*Konnichi-wa.*
Good Evening.	*Kon ban wa.*
Good Night.	*Oyasumi nasai.*
Hello (When answering the telephone)	*Moshi moshi.*
Goodbye.	*Sayonara.*
Cheers.	*Com paii.*
Oh, yes.	*Ah so.*
How are you?	*Ogenki desuka?*
I'm fine.	*Genki desu.*
Thank you.	*Ari gato.*
Thank you very much.	*Ari gato Gozaimasu.*
You're welcome.	*Doi tashi mashite.*
Yes.	*Hai.*
No.	*Iie.*
Water.	*Mizu.*
Hot.	*At sui.*
Cold.	*Sa mui.*
Welcome.	*Yokoso.*
Nice to meet you.	*Ha ji memashite.*
Do you speak Japanese?	*Nihongo o hanoshi masuka?*
Please.	*Dozo.*

Do you understand?

I understand.

I do not understand.

I am sorry.

Excuse me.

How do you do?

I am glad to meet you.

Just a moment please.

Mr./Mrs./Miss/Ms. Watanabe.

Friend.

Happy New Year

What time is it?

Happy Birthday.

How much is this?

I had a good time. Thank you very much.

It's very nice.

What is your name?

Waka ri masuka?

Waka ri mas.

Waka ri masen.

Gomen nasai.

Sumi masen.

Ha ji me mashite?

Dozo yoro shiku.

Chotto matte kudasai.

Watanabe-san.

Tomodachi.

Akemashite Omedeto Gozaimasu.

Ima nanji desuka?

Otanjobi Omedeto Gozaimasu.

Kore wa ikura desuka?

Tanoshi katta domo arigato.

Totemo ii kimochi desu.

Anata no na ma e wa nan desuka?

Sources

Canon, Inc., (1988). Exploring Japan.

Japan Travel Bureau, Inc., (1993). A Look into Japan.

Japan Travel Bureau, Inc., (1994). Japanese Family and Culture.

The Linguaphone Institute. (1968) Linguaphone Institute Limited, London. Japanese Course Book.

Montessori, M. (1964). The Montessori Method. Schocken Books, Inc.

A Guide for Book Clubs or Reading Groups

Dear Readers:

Thank you very much for purchasing my book. I hope you have enjoyed reading it as much as I enjoyed living the experience, recounting it and then writing about it.

The following questions have been designed to help you reflect, ponder and continue discussions around issues relating to family, culture, ethnicity and race.

◆　　　◆　　　◆

1. Do you think that Stephanie was acting irresponsibly, being irrational or impulsive by venturing out on her own and traveling with her young son to a foreign country where she had no family or friends?

2. Fear and anxiety are a recurring theme in the book. Why was Stephanie afraid; what was she afraid of; and did she eventually conquer her fear? And if so, how?

3. When Stephanie states that in Japan she and Christopher represented their *country,* whereby in the U.S. they represented their *ethnicity,* what did she mean by that? Also, why are race and ethnicity such a hot topic and a major issue in the U.S.?

4. Stephanie often discusses culture shock. Have you ever experienced culture shock in your own country or while visiting another country? If so, what was your experience and how did you feel?

5. Stephanie and Christopher went from culture shock to cultural learning and cultural understanding. What is your understanding of that?

6. Stephanie stated that Christopher was a child who struggled with transition and change. However, he seemed to adapt quite well to life in Japan. How does that experience speak to his adaptability and his resilience?

7. Stephanie wrote that she went to Japan for herself; however, she returned to the U.S. for her son. What did she mean by that?

8. Given the opportunity, would *you* have done what Stephanie did—sublet your apartment, sell your car, sell your furniture, pack your bags and take your young child and venture out into "unknown territory?"

9. What are some of the "lessons learned" by Stephanie and Christopher?

10. What do you think would have been the result of Stephanie and Christopher staying on in Japan for another year or more?

978-0-595-37698-8
0-595-37698-3

www.ingramcontent.com/pod-product-compliance
Lightning Source LLC
Chambersburg PA
CBHW020438290526
45785CB00002B/905

* 9 780595 376988 *